INSTRUCTOR'S MANUAL

to Accompany

Essentials of Psychology

Spencer A. Rathus

prepared by

Patricia P. Gadban

Holt, Rinehart and Winston

New York Chicago San Francisco Philadelphia
Montreal Toronto London Sydney
Tokyo Mexico City Rio de Janeiro Madrid

ISBN 0-03-069872-3

CBS COLLEGE PUBLISHING
Holt, Rinehart and Winston
The Dryden Press
Saunders College Publishing

CONTENTS

THE TEXTBOOK

The Rathus package for teaching introductory psychology begins with a textbook that is easily understood, interest-arousing, clearly written, succinct in presentation, well-illustrated, comprehensive and balanced, and applied as well as theoretical. The package is rounded out with an Instructor's Manual, a Student Study Guide, a Test Bank, a Computerized Test Bank and a Slide Program. Careful attention has been paid to each element of the set in an attempt to provide you, the instructor, with a highly integrated and efficient set of materials to ensure that you and your students have a successful teaching and learning experience.

THE INSTRUCTOR'S MANUAL

The Instructor's Manual is a careful blend of familiar and unique elements designed to help the instructor organize subject matter for effective classroom presentation and motivate students so that the introductory psychology course will become one of the students' most memorable learning experiences. Introductory material in the Instructor's Manual includes information on test construction and use of films in the classroom. Then each chapter of the Instructor's Manual corresponds to a chapter of the textbook and the complementary Study Guide. Each chapter of the Instructor's Manual is divided into the following sections: Learning Objectives (which parallel the learning objectives listed in the student Study Guide); Lecture Notes, which provide one complete full-period lecture for a major topic within each chapter; Discussion Questions; and Materials for Student Distribution. The Instructor's Manual also includes a lengthy package of materials called The Whole Psychology Catalogue: A Potpourri of New Items, Activities, Projects, Questionnaires, and Classroom Demonstrations. This unique catalogue will help make introductory psychology a vivid and well-remembered experience for students.

STUDY GUIDE

The Study Guide also blends the familiar and the unique. Each of its chapters corresponds to a chapter in the text and contains time-tested elements to motivate students and aid in retention of subject matter; a chapter Overview, which serves as an advance organizer (a chapter outline is already placed at the beginning of each chapter in the text itself); a list of Learning Objectives; a list of Key Terms; one or two Exercises that often involve matching concepts; a fill-in-the-blanks Chapter Review; and three 20-item multiple-choice Practice Tests. This total of sixty multiple-choice items per chapter is unmatched by any other introductory psychology study guide. In addition, the Study Guide contains two unique sections: Test Anxiety and Aiming Toward a Career in Psychology. The section on test anxiety reports research concerning origins and correlates of test anxiety, and suggests methods in keeping with recent research that students may use in an effort to cope with their test anxiety. This may be an invaluable aid to them in other college courses as well. The section on careers supplements the discussion in Chapter 1 of the text on specialties within psychology. It indicates licensing and certification requirements in the various states, and provides hints for getting into graduate school. Perhaps more important, this section recognizes that there are many opportunities to engage in psychological work at less-than-doctoral levels, and provides information about careers in psychology at the associate's, bachelor's, and master's degree levels, as well as at the doctoral level.

TEST BANK

The Test Bank contains more than 2,000 multiple-choice items. Above each item is a set of codes which indicate text page number and whether the item tests knowledge or application.

COMPUTERIZED TEST BANK

The Computerized Test Bank is available to instructors who adopt the text and provides you with a resource that is more efficient than the personalized test-typing service offered by some publishers. Once you have had the disks delivered to your college or university computer center, you need only supply the center with the numbers of the items you wish to use. Your own on-campus center can then supply you with printed tests in the numbers you specify within a matter of hours. There is no need for long-distance phone calls, no need to be concerned about delays in the mails.

SLIDE PROGRAM

The Slide Program that is also available to adopters of the textbook completes the Rathus package and will help you present information beyond the text. Descriptions of each slide, suggestions for use in class, and outside references are provided in the Resource Guide, which accompanies the slides.

A great deal of thought and work has gone into the Rathus package. We believe that the package, like the text, is interest-arousing, comprehensive and well-balanced, and represents the applied as well as the theoretical approach. It is meant to serve as a familiar yet unique package that will help lighten the load and increase the enjoyment of introductory psychology students.

USING THE INSTRUCTOR'S MANUAL

This manual contains a variety of materials that will facilitate your teaching of introductory psychology. Following this section you will find a sample syllabus for the course, which may be distributed to students once you have modified it to meet your own instruction needs. Then there are sections on constructing tests and on use of films in the classroom. All films on the list have been previewed by Holt, Rinehart and Winston authors, and it is believed that each has something to offer the introductory psychology student. The film section is presented early to remind you that films must usually be ordered well in advance of intended usage; some audiovisual departments require that films on hand be reserved one month in advance, and it is often recommended that three months be allowed for receipt of films that are being rented from outside agencies.

A CHAPTER-BY-CHAPTER APPROACH

The heart of the Instructor's Manual is organized by chapters to correspond to the Rathus text. Chapters contain the following sections:

1. Learning Objectives
   These objectives correspond to objectives listed in the student Study Guide and are designed to help students know what they are supposed to learn from the chapter. They have been reproduced here so that you will be more fami-

2

liar with information available to your students, and to provide a checklist of whether you have covered the main points in a classroom discussion.

2. Lecture Notes

For each chapter, lecture notes for a full-period lecture on a major topic have been provided. Each of these lectures has been used in the classroom, and I have attempted to provide information concerning feedback from students, points that may need extra efforts at clarification--even occasional attempts at humor. In each case, I have found that the material can be covered in approximately fifty minutes, allowing some time throughout the discussion for student questions and comments.

3. Discussion Questions

A number of topics were chosen as discussion questions because they may serve as interest-arousing lead-ins for discussion of a certain topic, because students may already hold strong opinions about them, or because they apply many of the implications of the text. They are quite varied, and some are quite controversial. I have used most of these questions in my classes and, when possible, I have tried to indicate what types of statements or subjects are commonly misinterpreted by students, especially since students occasionally have a way of assuming that an instructor who raises a certain topic for discussion--such as the issue of whether rape is a victim-precipitated crime-- is somehow endorsing the point of view being raised.

4. Materials for Student Distribution

This section corresponds to materials in the Whole Psychology Catalogue, which is the final section of the Instructor's Manual. In the Materials for Student Distribution section within each chapter, suggestions are made for using the items in the catalogue. These suggestions may include ways of introducing the materials, or of integrating them into classroom discussions and demonstrations. Occasionally it is indicated that materials may be used to illustrate discussion pertinent to more than one chapter. New clippings from sources such as TIME magazine and the NEW YORK TIMES have been selected because of relevance to class discussions. For the great majority of students, future exposure to psychology will be in the form of such articles or in the form of television discussion of psychological findings and issues. These articles and discussions tend to be laden with inaccuracies, and it may be that instructors can do their students a great service by "ripping apart" a few such articles with their students, in order to teach them to be skeptical and wary in their future reading.

News clippings in the catalogue are not necessarily accurate. They have been chosen because of their relevance to topics discussed in introductory psychology. For this reason the following warning is presented after the first news item listed in the Materials for Student Distribution section of each chapter.

New items presented in these handouts may be abbreviated versions of the originals, but they have not been otherwise altered. Thus it is advised that instructors read them carefully to determine whether certain statements are scientifically unsound and should thus receive commentary in the classroom.

THE WHOLE PSYCHOLOGY CATALOGUE

The Whole Psychology Catalogue is the final section of this Instructor's Manual. It is indeed a "potpourri" of news items, projects, activities, questionnaires, and materials for use in classroom demonstrations.

COURSE OUTLINE AND SYLLABUS FOR RATHUS' PSYCHOLOGY

The syllabi used by some instructors cover precisely the main points of a course in outline form. It may do no more than repeat the contents of the textbook and, perhaps, indicate a date by which a student should be prepared to discuss or take an examination on a certain chapter or group of chapters.

For other instructors a "syllabus" states course policies (for example, what to do when a test is missed), test dates, grading procedures, including the number and percentage of available points needed in order to achieve a certain grade level, and other information such as a description of term paper topics, how to earn extra credit, or outside sources of information, or a reading list.

I like to put as much information into a syllabus as possible, especially clear statements about grading procedures and course policies. A well-written syllabus relieves students of anxiety that stems from ambiguity. It also avoids the problems of students failing the course because they did not know when tests were going to be given, how to arrange for make-ups, how many points were needed to pass the course, and so on. This information also protects you from student complaints at the end of the course. If you have provided a written statement about grading and course policies, a student cannot later complain that he or she has never been advised or warned about these matters.

Here is a sample syllabus for an introductory psychology course constructed around the Rathus text:

Fall Term, 1984

PSYCHOLOGY 101--Introduction to Psychology

(Section 3--Period 3--MWF)

Instructor:	I. M. Youneek
Office:	Psychology Building--Room 341
Office Hours:	MWF: 11:00-12:00
	TTh: 9:30-10:30
Office Phone:	437-3327
Required Text:	Rathus, S. A. ESSENTIALS OF PSYCHOLOGY, New York: Holt, Rinehart and Winston, 1986
Recommended:	Rathus, S. A. Self-Scoring Study Guide for Essentials of Psychology, New York: Holt, Rinehart and Winston.
Course Objectives:	1. A primary objective of any introductory course is to provide you with the concepts and vocabulary of the subject matter in the field of study. The primary purpose of Psychology 101 is

4

to introduce you to the science of psychology by familiarizing you with important psychological concepts, research findings, and basic principles of behavior.

2. A second major objective of Psychology 101 is to replace the popular image of psychology with a more accurate picture of the nature and content areas of psychology.

Course
Outline:

Chapter 1 What Is Psychology? (An Introduction to Psychology as a Science)
Chapter 2 Biology and Behavior
Chapter 3 Sensation and Perception

FIRST EXAM: September 17--Chapters 1-3

Chapter 4 Learning and Cognition
Chapter 5 Motivation and Emotion

SECOND EXAM: October 8--Chapters 4-5

Chapter 6 Developmental Psychology
Chapter 7 Personality

THIRD EXAM: October 29--Chapters 6-7

Chapter 8 Abnormal Behavior
Chapter 9 Psychological assessment of Personality and Intelligence

FOURTH EXAM: November 19--Chapters 10-11

Chapter 10 Psychotherapy
Chapter 11 Social Psychology

FINAL EXAM: December 17--Questions will cover the entire course, with special emphasis on Chapters 10 and 11

Course
Requirements:

1. As you can see from the course outline, there are four (4) regularly scheduled exams plus the final examination. Each of the four regular exams will consist of fifty (50) multiple-choice questions worth two (2) points each for a total of one hundred points per exam. Most items will be based on reading assignments, but some questions may also be drawn from class discussions or films. The final exam will consist of one hundred (100) multiple-choice questions worth two (2) points each. Thus the final exam is worth the equivalent of two regularly scheduled exams, or one-third of the course grade.

2. Make-up exams will be given only for very serious reasons (for example, real illnesses or deaths in your family). If you miss one of the regularly scheduled exams for an appropriately serious reason, you will be required to make it up during the last regularly scheduled class period (December 14). NO MAKE-UP EXAMS WILL BE GIVEN AT ANY OTHER TIMES FOR ANY REASON. No more than one missed exam may be made up.

Grading:

1. Grades will be based on points earned on the four regularly scheduled exams and the final exam. Each of the regularly scheduled exams counts for one-sixth of your grade, and the final exam counts for one-third.

2. The following grade scale will be used for each 50-item exam to let you know where you stand on each test:

   a. If you get 90-100 points, your grade is A;
   b. If you get 80-88 points, your grade is B;
   c. If you get 70-78 points, your grade is C;
   d. If you get 60-68 points, your grade is D;
   e. If you get below 60 points, your grade is F.

3. For the final exam, simply double the number of points required for each letter grade in the above examples.

4. Your final grade will be determined by adding up the total number of points you earned on the four regularly scheduled exams plus the final exam. Thus:

   a. If you have a total of 540-600 points,
      your final grade is A;
   b. If you have a total of 480-538 points
      your final grade is B;
   c. If you have a total of 420-478 points,
      your final grade is C;
   d. If you have a total of 360-418 points,
      your final grade is D;
   e. If your total is below 360 points,
      your final grade is F.

Cheating: Anyone caught cheating at any time during the term will receive an automatic F for this course.

I have seen statements like the following included on syllabi from time to time, and present them here in case instructors feel that one or more of them might be useful additions to their own syllabi:

"Students missing an exam must notify me in writing within five class days following the exam, and must have an acceptable excuse. Medical excuses require a doctor's letter."

"If a student misses an exam with an unacceptable excuse, the student will receive zero (0) credit for the exam, which will be averaged in like any other grade. The letter grade of F will not be averaged in instead."

"Students who feel that they do not do well on multiple-choice questions will not be permitted alternative ways of earning grades."

"Students who wish to take the course on a Pass/Fail basis must notify the instructor prior to taking the first exam, and not after earning a couple of D's and a C!"

A GUIDE TO TEST CONSTRUCTION

The preparation of good test questions is a technique that is fairly easily learned, but without it both time and effort can be wasted, and resulting tests will not be as useful as they could be. The following hints may appear either naive or hair-splitting, but they have proved to be of value to many instructors.

The Planning Stage: Questions to Consider in Planning a Test

1. What skills, knowledge, attitudes, and so forth, do I want to test? Perhaps the single most important part of constructing a series of questions occurs before the first question is formulated. Its essence is to stop thinking of Chapter X, or whatever unit you are testing, and to start thinking of the student who has studied it. What should he or she have learned? What factual knowledge should have been acquired? Can the student apply this knowledge? What is important . . . and what is not so important? Unless you are a very experienced test instructor, the fact that you are familiar with the subject matter does not mean that you have the answers to these questions at your fingertips. But until you do you will not know concretely what mastery of that chapter implies; you will not know what the questions should be trying to do. This analysis of what test constructors call the "behavioral objectives" of the chapter can remain in your head, but it may be more useful to put them down on paper and make them specific enough to be expressed in percentages of the whole.

2. What proportions should the test have? The next step is to translate the list of priorities into a "mix" of questions that reflects these priorities. First, determine the percentages that you will allot to the different subjects or skills that are prerequisites of mastery; next translate these into percentages of questions. If you have decided that factual recall of the details of this or that is most important, then your decision will probably be that, say, 50 percent of the questions will be devoted to this area. If that is not the case you may warn yourself that not more than, say, 25 percent should involve factual recall. Having this proportional prescription in front of you is like buying a map before you set out on a journey; it will warn you when you are spending too much time and trouble on one section of the chapter and will continually point out to you the next area of concentration.

3. What types of test items will best do the job? Specifying the proportion of test items to meet each of the behavioral objectives is only half the battle. We still have to select the appropriate types of questions for the different jobs. To give a simple example, if it is important that the student be able to organize his or her ideas about a complex topic, an essay question (or essay questions) would be more appropriate. If mastery of technical vocabulary is an important objective, perhaps a short-answer format would be best. We will discuss the advantages and limitations of each type

of test question as we consider them one by one. But the following tabular summary of their general characteristics may be useful (++ is very useful; -- is useless.)

FACTOR	ESSAY	SHORT- ANSWER	TRUE-FALSE, MATCHING, MULTIPLE-CHOICE
Measures student's ability to select, organize, and express ideas	++	+	-
Discourages bluffing	--	-	++
Potential diagnositc value	--	-	++
Answer cannot be deduced by process of elimination	++	++	-
Scoring is reliable	--	-	++
Independent of fluency	--	+	++
Provides for good item pool	--	+	++
Takes relatively little time to prepare	++	+	-
Measures higher mental processes	++	-	++
Provides for broad content sampling	--	+	++
Measures application in novel situations	++	+	++
Provides for adequate sampling of objectives	--	+	++
Measures originality	++	+	--

As a result of going through this planning stage, the different proportions and subject matters of the four varieties of test questions will emerge; you will acquire a blue print of what you do. There is, however, one unsettled question remaining:

4. How difficult should the questions be? The majority of test items in a study guide and test bank are for diagnostic or mastery purposes. They are not intended to establish who knows the material best; if the test is a valid one—if it really tests mastery of the chapter—it would be perfectly acceptable if everyone achieved the same score.

Mastery tests should be difficult enough to exercise the student and easy enough for the majority to do well. Discriminatory tests should be constructed so that about half the students will probably answer the questions incorrectly. In this way you can expect a wide spread of scores, which is a desirable result of a discriminatory test.

The mix of questions for a particular chapter should conform to the needs of that chapter. This mix can be identical for all chapters (a certain number of essay questions, so many multiple-choice, so many short-answer, and so on) only if the demands of all chapters are identical. The habit of establishing a pattern of questions and sticking to it is not necessarily a good one.

The Essay Question

The essay question can come in more forms that most people realize. The first distinction to be made is between the extended response and restricted response types. In the former virtually no bounds are placed upon the student, who literally writes an essay. The latter specifies the length of the answer—usually one page or less—and, if there is any possibility of ambiguity, what aspect(s) of the problem should be discussed.

The restricted essay is easier and more reliable to score and quicker to administer. But it limits the opportunity for the student to synthesize his or her ideas and express them in a logical, coherent form. Because of this the restricted response form is of greater value for measuring the student's ability to comprehend, analyze, and apply what has been learned, while the extended essay questions test synthesis and evaluation better.

From the point of view of form, the essay question can be of many varieties.

Comparison of two or more things or concepts

Decision for or against a statement

Causes or effects

> Ex.: Why did subjects in the Asch studies conform to inaccurate group judgments?

Explanation of the exact meaning or use of a phrase or statement in a passage

Analysis

> Ex.: Does the inappropriate resolution of the Oedipus complex suffice as an explanation of homosexual behavior? Support your answer with research evidence.

Statement of relationships

> Ex.: Why does validity imply reliability but not the converse?

Discussion

> Ex.: Discuss Pavlov's experiments in classical conditioning.

9

Reorganization of facts

>Ex.: Trace the development of sexual attitudes on Mangaia as compared with those on Inis Baeg.

Formulation of new question (problems and questions raised)

>Ex.: Assume that a disease made all people color-blind, but we still needed to perceive differences in color. Can you think of a way in which electronic devices could be used to supplement the human sensory apparatus?

Criticism (as to the adequacy, correctness, or relevancy of a printed statement)

It would, incidentally, be a useful exercise to decide which of these forms would be more suited for the restricted or the extended response form.

The general rules for writing essay questions are both simple and fairly obvious.

1. The question should elicit the behavior you want. If you want opinions, make that clear. Ex.: "Do you think abortion can be justified as moral?" If you want the facts, say so. Ex.: "Compare the advantages and disadvantages of three methods of abortion."

2. Delimit the area covered by the questions. Assume, as you should in every aspect of test writing, that students will misinterpret you if they possibly can. If you want a description of classical conditioning, specify whether you want students to define classical conditioning and terms like US, LS, and so forth.

3. Use descriptive words. "Define, outline, classify, summarize" are reasonably clear in their meaning. "Discuss," on the other hand, needs to be delimited by specific instructions as to what points should be discussed.

4. "Aim" the student at the desired response. A well-composed essay questions may result in the students not knowing the answer but knowing exactly what it is that he or she does not know. Do not be afraid of long essay questions if they are necessary to define what type of answer you are seeking exactly. This advice applies particularly to the restricted-response type of essay question.

Objective Tests in General

There are several rules that apply to all objective tests.

1. Test for important facts and knowledge. "Important" depends on your evaluation of the behavioral objectives of the chapter. But do not necessarily be tempted by a concrete fact that appears in the chapter just because it lends itself to a short-answer question. Knowledge of that fact may or may not be of relevance to mastery of the chapter.

2. Write the items as clearly as possible. This is the same general principle that was discussed in regard to essay questions: If students can misinterpret a question, they will. For example, "The first psychology laboratory was established in _____." can be answered correctly by the date, the year, or the name of the university

or nation. "The first psychology laboratory was established in the year _____."
pins the student down.

3. Whenever possible use quantitative language. This is really an extension of the
    previous principle. "Lot," "few," "many," and "low" mean different things to dif-
    ferent people. Specify.

4. Avoid lifting statements verbatim from the text. To do so runs the risk of ambi-
    guity by removal of the context and encourages the student to memorize rather
    than understand.

5. Avoid using interrelated items. These are series of questions in which the correct
    answer to one is necessary to get the correct answer to another. They are usually
    computational questions, and can underestimate the mastery of the student.

6. Avoid negative questions whenever possible. Negative questions add an unneces-
    sary complexity to the student's thought processes, and "catching him (or her)"
    because of this is usually irrelevant to your purposes. And if negatives are to
    be avoided, double negatives should be doubly avoided. When you do use negatives,
    be sure to call attention to them by placing the negative in italics or capitals.

7. Do not give the answer away. There are several ways in which this can happen:

    Having information in the stem of one question that provides the answer
    to another question.

    Lacking parallelism between stem and responses in multiple-choice items.

    Making the correct multiple-choice longer than the incorrect ones.

    Following a pattern of "true" and "false" or of position in multiple-choice
    questions.

    Using grammatical hints such as "a" and "an".

    Using textbook language verbatim.

    Using technical jargon.

8. Don't be cute or funny or trivial. A regrettable number of test constructors--per-
    haps because they get bored with the job--insert "funny" or ridicuIuous alternatives
    in multiple-choice questions. Their excuse, if asked, will probably be that they
    are out to catch the blind guesser or to entertain students. But the practice dimi-
    nishes the number of plausible alternatives and may lower the student's opinion
    of the test constructor.

    A similar but more unfair practice is to try to catch the student with minor
    errors of spelling and so on in the responses. It is more useful to test the student's
    mastery than his or her proofreader's eye.

Short-Answer Questions

The short-answer question lies midway between the restricted essay question and the
objective test proper. It asks the student to supply rather than to recognize the correct

answer. Because they are akin to essay questions, imprecise wording is to be particularly avoided. For example. "The originator of psychoanalysis was _____." can be answered perfectly correctly by "raised in Europe" (and you can be sure that some students will do so.) The question should be phrased: "The name of the originator of psychoanalysis is _____."

Remember that the traditional completion type of short-answer question is not the only form. We can say: "The first experimental psychology laboratory was located in the city of (Leipzig)." However, we can also be simpler: "In what city was the first experimental psychology laboratory situated?" (Leipzig).

In addition, we can use what is known as the "associational" type:

> After each form of therapy, write in the name of the originator of the form of therapy.

Psychosurgery	Moniz
Rational-emotive therapy	Ellis
Systematic desensitization	Wolpe

The following are some things to watch out for in writing short-answer questions.

1. In computational problems, specify the degree of precision and the units of expression.

2. Omit important words only.

3. Avoid excessive blanks in a single item. What is explicit to the tester must be equally explicit to the student. It is distressingly easy for a test constructor with something specific in mind to compose a short-answer question that becomes merely a guessing game. For a reductio ad absurdum, what are the missing words in this question?

> The ratio of the _____ to the _____ is called the _____.

Of course, nobody would write a question like that. Or would they?

4. Put the blanks near the end of the sentence. The blank is the question; the student should be able to focus his or her mind on it when the rest of the "work" of reading the question has been done. Rereading the question to make sure of what is wanted should not be necessary.

5. Where possible, use the direct question rather than the incomplete sentence. The direct question is not only more natural to the student, but also lends itself better to the elimination of ambiguity and irrelevant clues. Surprisingly, many test constructors fail to consider the "legitimacy" of a direct question format in a short-answer question. But it is just as correct to say: "In what year was the first psychology laboratory established? _____" as it is to say: "The first psychology laboratory was established in the year ____."--and frequently a great deal simpler. This format applies particularly to tests of the knowledge of technical terms.

6. Do not skimp on the answer space provided. At the same time, do not provide

12

clues to the answer by the length of the space. It is good practice to make all spaces the same length, enough to accommodate the longest answer.

Matching Questions

There are two variants of the traditional double-column matching question that can be used with advantage on occasion. In the first a diagram or map is presented with locations or parts assigned letters or numbers. The student matches these letters or numbers with a list supplied with the question. In the second variety a set of statements and a numbered classification scheme are presented, and the student assigns a classification to each statement. This variation is well suited to topics dealing with criticism, explanation, or understanding.

The matching exercise has the advantage of requiring little reading time and consequently making it possible to sample a large amount of a chapter's content. On the other hand, its format tends to encourage rote memorization rather than association, and it may be difficult to provide clusters of questions that are sufficiently alike for a common set of responses to be used.

The following are some suggestions for the constructor of a set of matching questions.

1. Response list items should be short and on the right. The longer questions, or statements to be classified, should be read first, for which the left side is normal. The short responses then need only be scanned to select the appropriate one.

2. Each matching exercise should consist of homogeneous items. This is easier said than done, because homogeneity is not an absolute concept; there are levels of homogenity, and the appropriate one should be aimed for. And the finer the discrimination to be made by the student, the more demanding the criterion of homogeneity and the more difficult it will be to supply homogeneous items.

3. Keep each list relatively short. The ordinary range should be from five to twelve items, with five to eight the optimum.

4. Avoid having an equal number of premises and responses. A good rule of thumb is to have two or three more responses than premises. It is also a good idea to list responses that can be used once, more than once, or not at all. This forms an effective anti-guessing device.

5. Arrange the responses in some systematic fashion. Random listing of the responses may needlessly complicate the task for the student; the simpler the question the more effective a test it provides. Words may be in alphabetical order; dates and numbers in ascending or descending order.

6. Explain clearly the basis on which the match is to be made. If one column is types of therapy and the other names of therapists, does the student match the therapy types with the practitioners or vice versa? If it is to be a one-to-one match it does not matter, but if one list has items to be used once, more than once, or not at all, confusion can result. Tell the student explicitly what is to be done and how it is to be done.

7. Maintain grammatical consistency. Use all proper names or all common nouns;

all singulars or all plurals, all men or all women. Mixing lists may provide irrelevant clues.

8. Every response should be a plausible answer to every premise. This is the most obvious, the more important, and, probably, the hardest rule to follow.

True-False Questions

True-false questions have fallen into a certain amount of ill-repute, but this is probably because the apparent ease of constructing them forms an invitation to carelessness. While it may be true that some of the worst objective tests are composed of true-false questions, it is also true that true-false questions can do as good a job of checking mastery or discriminating between students as any other type of objective test.

Some suggestions in writing true-false questions follow.

1. Ambiguity and lack of clarity are both easy and fatal in true-false questions. As we have mentioned, this particularly applies to the use of indefinite quantitatives, such as "more," "less," "few", "heavier," and the like. Different people interpret these terms in different ways; use specific numerical terms whenever possible.

2. A true-false question must be wholly true or wholly false. Do not include a true clause in a sentence that is to be marked "false." Which part of the sentence determines the answer? An associated problem is the sentence that is not wholly true or wholly false, or that is true only some of the time or under special circumstances. You may consider the occasional use of a three-way answer: T, F, S, "true," "false," "sometimes."

    Yet another variant is the statement that is true only within a certain frame of reference. This can be solved by specifying the frame. For example: "The limits of borderline intelligence are 70-79 IQ" is unambiguously true only when a further specification is added: The limits of borderline intelligence are 70-79 IQ on the WAIS (Wechsler Adult Intelligence Scale)."

3. Avoid trick questions. The slight misspelling of a name, the substitution of B.C. for A.D. in a date, a word "almost but not quite" right, and so on, may catch a few students who read too quickly, but do not necessarily assess mastery of the subject matter. Students should not be penalized for being under pressure.

4. If a true-false question is in a cause-and-effect form, make the cause correct (and tell the student so) and leave the true-false judgment for the effect. This arrangement should be made clear to the student. For example: "Whites outscore blacks on standardized IQ tests" (true) "because white parents encourage their children to practice these tests" (true or false?).

5. Word the statement so that superficial knowledge suggests a wrong answer. Avoid specific determiners. This fault is frequently a by-product of an attempt to make sure that the statement is wholly true the test writer will qualify the statement by words such as "usually," "should," or "some," while with false statements the opposite occurs--"never," "none," or "all." The test-wise student quickly catches on to this pattern and will answer correctly without knowing anything about the subject.

14

6. Avoid making true statements consistently longer than false statements. Another irrelevant clue.

7. Have approximately the same number of true and false statements. Exactly the same number may provide clues to test-wise students.

Multiple-Choice Questions

Multiple-choice questions are undoubtedly the most popular form of objective test. The popularity of the multiple-choice question is deserved, for several reasons. They are versatile and can test many aspects of a student's mastery. They are relatively efficient, and their difficulty can be controlled by varying the degree of homogeneity of the responses. They are not easy to guess but at the same time are preferred by students to both short-answer and true-false items. Finally, of all selection-type objective questions, multiple-choice questions are most free from the influence of response sets--the tendency of the individual to give a different answer to the same content when the form of the question is varied.

At the same time, multiple-choice questions have limitations, real or potential. They are difficult to construct, and test constructors may have a temptation to confine them to items of factual recall. They take longer to answer than other forms of objective tests. Finally, the multiple-choice question favors the test-wise student.

The advantages of multiple-choice questions can be maximized and the defects minimized by observing the following points.

1. The essence of the problem should be in the stem. The student should know exactly what is expected and be formulating an answer by the time the options are read. A simple test of this is to cover up the options and read the stem as if it were a short-answer question--if the stem is properly written it should work as one.

2. Avoid repetition of words in the options. The key words should all be incorporated in the stem. Doing so saves the student reading time and focuses attention on the problem.

3. Avoid superfluous wording. A question is not necessarily improved by elaboration.

4. When the incomplete-statement format is used, the options should come at the end of the statement. This is in line with the general principle that the problem should be presented quickly and easily.

5. Arrange the alternatives as simply as possible. The responses should be arranged in a column below the stem, in some apparent order--alphabetical, by ascending or descending order, or by length of response.

6. Avoid technical distracters. Test constructors frequently are tempted to add to the difficulty of the question by unfamiliar or difficult vocabulary. This violates the general principle that the content and not the format of the question is the test.

7. All responses should be plausible and homogeneous. One of the advantages of the multiple-choice question is that it reduces the probability of guessing the correct answer, by making it necessary to choose among several alternatives.

If we throw away some of these alternatives by making some responses obviously implausible, we are rendering the question less functional than it could be.

8. Avoid making the correct response longer than the incorrect ones. If qualifiers have to be used in the correct response to ensure its correctness, you should go back and insert qualifiers in the distracters to even up the lengths. The longest response is an obvious choice for guessers.

9. Avoid giving irrelevant clues to the correct answer. We have discussed this in relation to other types of objective tests. Some ways in which this mistake may be made are (a) the use of "a" or "an" in an incomplete statement form (if the grammatical needs of the responses differ, use "a(n)"); (b) asking the name of a male and having most of the distracters female; and (c) having a conflict between singular and plural in the stem and the options.

10. Be cautious in using "all of the above" as an option. This is especially true when the question is constructed so that "all of the above" is the correct response. In a typical four-option question, this means that the student who recognizes that two of the responses are correct can pick "all of the above" and score as if he or she knew the complete answer. If you use "all of the above" as a correct option, be sure to instruct students to consider all the choices before they record their responses.

11. Use the "none of the above" option sparingly. The use of "none of the above" should be limited to cases where the student is convinced that it is a possible option and not a distracter, and to cases where the correct response is absolutely correct.

12. Use three to five options. There is no law that says that the same number of options has to be used for every question. Three is the minimum for a multiple-choice question; more than five is not only difficult to construct but unnecessary. It is perfectly good practice to vary from three to five options depending upon the question. "All" or "none of the above" is commonly used as a fifth option.

CHECKLISTS FOR TEST CONSTRUCTION

To save you time, the suggestions we have provided for writing different forms of test questions have been combined into a series of checklists. You may find it useful to run your eyes over them after completing a batch of questions.

Checklist for Writing Essay Questions

---

1. Is the question restricted to measuring objectives that would not be assessed more efficiently by other item formats?
2. Does each question relate to some instructional objective?
3. Does the question establish a framework to guide the student to the expected answer?
   a) Is the problem delimited?
   b) Are descriptive words such as "compare," "contrast," and "define" used rather than words such as "discuss" or "explain"?
   c) For the restricted-response essay in particular, is the student "aimed" to the answer by appropriate subdivisions of the main questions?

4. Are the questions novel? Do they challenge the student? Do they require the student to demonstrate originality of thought and expression?*
5. Are the questions realistic in terms of:
   a) difficulty?
   b) time allowed the student to respond?
   c) complexity of the task?
6. Are all students expected to answer the same questions?
7. Is there a preponderance of short-answer (restricted-response) questions?
*Originality need not be an objective for every question.

Checklist for Writing Objective Test Items

FACTOR

1. Are the instructional objectives clearly defined?
2. Did you prepare a test blueprint? Did you follow it?
3. Did you formulate well-defined, clear test items?
4. Did you employ "correct" English in writing the items"
5. Did you specifically state all necessary qualifications?
6. Did you avoid giving clues to the correct answer? For example, grammatical clues, length of correct response clues?
7. Did you test for the important ideas rather than the trivial?
8. Did you adapt the test's difficulty to your students?
9. Did you avoid using textbook jargon?
10. Did you cast the items in positive form?
11. If negative items were used, did you draw the students' attention to them?
12. Does each and every item have a single correct answer?

Checklist for Writing Short-Answer (Supply Type) Items

FACTOR

1. Can each item be answered in a word, a phrase, a formula, or short sentence, with a symbol?
2. Do the items avoid the use of verbatim textbook language?
3. Is each item specific, clear, and unambiguous?
4. Are any irrelevant clues avoided? Grammatical? Length of blank? Other?
5. Do computational problems indicate the degree of precision required? Whether or not the unit of measurement is to be included in the answer?
6. Do blanks occur near the end of the sentence?
7. Have only key words been omitted?
8. Was excessive mutilation kept to a minimum?
9. Have direct questions been used where feasible?
10. Are the items technically correct?
11. Is there one correct or agreed-upon correct answer?
12. Is this format most efficient for testing the instructional objectives?

Checklist for Writing Matching Exercises

FACTOR

1. Have you given the student clear, explicit instructions?
2. Are the response and premise lists both homogeneous?
3. Is one list shorter than the other?
4. Are both lists between five and twelve entries?
5. Are the premises longer and more complex? The responses simple and short?
6. Did you arrange the responses in some systematic order?
7. Do both lists of the exercise appear on the same page?
8. Are your lists relatively free of clues?

Checklist for Writing True-False Items

FACTOR

1. Is each item expressed in clear, simple language?
2. Did you avoid lifting statements verbatim from the text?
3. Have negative statements been avoided where possible?
4. Have specific determiners such as "all," "may," "sometimes," been avoided?
5. Have double-barreled items (part true, part false) been avoided?
6. Have trick questions been removed?
7. Is each item clearly true or false?
8. Are there approximately the same number of true and false items?

Checklist for Writing Multiple-Choice Items

FACTOR

1. Has the item been clearly presented? Is the main problem in the stem? Has excess verbiage been eliminated?
2. Has the item been cast so that there is no repetition of key words or phrases for each option?
3. Do the options come at the end of the stem?
4. Have the responses been arranged in some systematic fashion, such as alphabetical or length of response?
5. Are all distracters plausible? Are the number of distracters related to the subject matter?
6. Have all irrelevant clues been avoided (grammatical, rote verbal association, length of correct answer, etc.)?

7. Are the correct answers randomly assigned throughout the test with approximate-ly equal frequency?
8. Has an "I don't know" option been considered?
9. Is there only one correct (or best) answer?
10. Has "all the above" been avoided?
11. Has the "none of these" option been used sparingly? Only when appropriate?
12. Have overlapping options been avoided?
13. Have negative statements been avoided? If used, has the negative been under-lined or written in capital letters?

FILMS

Films are valuable aids to the instructor of psychology. They take the student out of the lecture room and make psychological techniques, subjects, and issues vivid and meaningful. Through films students have the opportunity to meet important psycholo-gists and to observe them as they talk about and demonstrate their own research pro-jects.

Recommended Films

Some instructors are not familiar with many of the fine films that are available for classroom use. Often their own college and university film catalogues do not provide information that will be helpful in the film selection process. Sometimes the films in these catalogues are outdated or in poor condition. Often the subject matter is insufficiently described so that the instructor is, in effect, showing them blind and hoping that they will be relevant and effective.

The films listed in this manual are generally up to date in their subject matter, even though some date back to the 1950s and at least one to the late 1940s. Their subject matter is described so that the instructor will have a more reasonable basis for selection than the title alone.

The Film List

The following films are arranged according to the chapter of the Rathus text that they would logically accompany. Most of them may be ordered once without charge for purposes of previewing. In general, the audiovisual department of your college or uni-versity will know how to obtain these films and can also indicate how much advance time they will need in order to make their orders. However, a list of addresses of most of the commonly used film companies is placed at the end of the list for instructors who wish to contact the companies or distribution agents on their own.

Chapter 1: Psychology and Human Behavior

<u>Methodology: The Psychologist and the Experiment</u>. McGraw-Hill/CRM, color, 31 min.
Highlights two famous experiments: Schachter's "fear and affiliation" experi-ment and Riesen's research with visual-motor coordination in kittens. Discusses independent and dependent variables, control groups, random group assignment, and some basic statistical concepts.

Aspects of Behavior. McGraw–Hill/CRM, color, 31 min. Indicates how broad and di-- verse a field psychology is by showing a number of topics of current interest to psychologists.

The Nature of Science: Obtaining Facts. Coronet, color, 11 min. Demonstrates how the scientific method is more reliable than one's sensory impressions as a way of gathering data by using visual illusions.

Miss Goodall and the Wild Chimpanzees. Wolper, color, 28 min. Jane Goodall describes her own naturalistic–observation studies with chimpanzees in East Africa.

Landmarks in Psychology. Human Relations Media, color 39 min. A filmstrip that highlights the influence of the psychoanalytic, humanistic, behavioral, and inter- personal schools of evolution of modern psychology.

Chapter 2: Biology and Behavior

The Brain: Creating the Mental Elite. Document Associates, color. 22 min. Demon- strates major areas of brain research, such as chemical and electrical stimulation of the brain, and environmental conditioning. Introduces Diamond, John, Kretch, and Penfield.

Split–Brain Operation. NET, b/w, 13 min. Demonstrates the technique and effects of the operation in which the corpus callosum is severed.

The Autonomic Nervous System. International Film Bureau, color, 17 min. Shows how functioning of organs such as the stomach, bladder, and lungs are controlled by the sympathetic and parasympathetic divisions of the autonomic nervous system.

The Hidden Universe. McGraw–Hill/CRM, color, 16 min. Provides an overview of major functions of the brain, such as sensory perception, motor control, and memory. David Janssen hosts.

Classic Experiments in Behavioral Neuropsychology. Association Films, color, 22 min. Presents classic experiments in behavioral neuropsychology.

The Split Brain and Conscious Experience. Association Films, color, 17½ min. Presents rare and unusual glimpses of split–brain patients.

The Mind of Man. Indiana University, color, 199 min. An excellent film. Covers all aspects of relationships between brain and behavior from prenatal development through the life cycle.

I Had a Stroke. Filmakers Library, color, 28 min. A case study of woman's rehabilita- tion following a stroke. Shows regenerative functions and limits of the nervous system.

Divided Brain and Consciousness. Harcourt, Brace, Jovanovich, color, 22 min. Fine exposition of functions of the two cerebral hemispheres.

Genetic Defects: The Broken Code. Pennsylvania State University, color, 22 min. Fine
introduction to concepts of genetic engineering. (Does not contain recent findings
on recombinant DNA and gene splicing.)

Chapter 3: Sensation and Perception

The Sensory World. McGraw-Hill/CRM, color, 33 min. Investigates how sensations are
converted into perceptions. Demonstrates work of Jerome Lettvin and Wilder
Penfield. Contains striking visual illustrations.

A World to Perceive. NET Focus on Behavior Series, b/w, 28 min. Walk and Gibson
demonstrate their visual cliff experiments. Herman Witkins demonstrates the
"tilting room."

Visual Perception. ETS, color, 20 min. Hadley Cantril demonstrates three visual illusions at Princeton's Perception Demonstration Center: the Ames distorted
room, the rotating trapezoid, and the apparent movement of balloons that vary in
size and brightness.

Perception. Appleton-Century-Crofts, color, 15 min. Differentiates between sensation
and perception. Demonstrates several illusions: reversible staircase, phi pheno-
menon, Benham's top, color satisfaction, perceptual set, the trapezoidal window,
and figure-ground relationships.

An Introduction to Visual Illusions. Pyramid, color, 18 min. Presents more than twenty
visual illusions. Shows how the eye processes light energy, and how depth is perceived.

The Skin as a Sense Organ. International Film Bureau, color, 12 min. Shows sensory
receptors for warmth, cold, touch, and pain. Shows transmission of sensation
from receptors to the brain.

An Introduction to Acupuncture. Pyramid, color, 22 min. Traces the history of acupuncture. Demonstrates its use as an analgesic in surgical procedures.

Dr. Rhine Discusses ESP. CCM, Parts I & II, color, each 45 min. Dr. Rhine discusses
his work in ESP, attempting to clarify misconceptions, demonstrating current
research. The films, of course, are generally supportive of Rhine's controversial
points of view.

Visual Search in Driving. Pennsylvania State University, color, 21 min. Shows effects
of road conditions on eye movements while driving. Fine demonstration of research methodology in sensation and perception.

The Cochlear Nerve. The Media Guild, color, 21 min. Sophisticated laboratory demonstration of the physiology of hearing. Shows microelectrode techniques with
guinea pigs.

Patterns of Pain. Filmakers Library, color, 28 min. Shows treatment of pain through
hypnosis, biofeedback, drugs, acupuncture, and electrode implantation. (Consider
use for Chapter 4 also.)

Senses of Man. Indiana University, color, 18 min. Exposition of sensory receptors,
especially of the skin and the chemical senses.

Sleep and Dreaming in Humans. MAAJ Indiana University, Films at Frontiers and Psychological Inquiry Series, color, 14 min. Illustrates research techniques to study
sleep: stages of sleep, electrode placement, polygraph usage, REM sleep, and so
on.

The Sleepwatchers. McGraw-Hill, color, 25 min. Reviews recent studies of sleep and
dreaming, influencing dreams, effects of REM and deep sleep deprivation.

The Sleeping Brain. Pennsylvania State University, color, 23 min. Dr. Michael Jouvet
illustrates the techniques used to study the physiology of sleep.

To Sleep . . . Perchance to Dream. Indiana University, b/w, 30 min. Dr. William
Dement's 1966 classic on sleep and dreams. Excellent description but in need of
supplemen-tary theoretical updating.

Chapter 4: Learning and Cognition

Classical and Instrumental Conditioning, Harper & Row Media, color, 20 min. Demonstrates two kinds of conditioning. (Note: Prepare students by explaining that
instrumental conditioning is equivalent to operant conditioning, as it is termed in
the text.)

Observational Learning. Harper & Row Media, color 23 min. Robert Liebert demonstrates several instances of observational learning.

Learning. McGraw-Hill/CRM, color, 30 min. Explores interactions between instinctive
responses and learning.

The Skinner Revolution. Research Press Films, color 23 min. Sketches Skinner's life
and work. Interviews Skinner.

B. F. Skinner and Behavior Change: Research, Practice, and Promise. Research Press
Films, color, 45 min. Presents theory, research, and applications of Skinner's
behavioral approach. Philosophical and ethical issues are explored. Interviews
Skinner.

Pavlov: The Conditional Reflex. Films for the Humanities, b/w, 25 min. A USSR
Central Television production explores Pavlov's findings on conditioning. Contains
historical footage of Pavlov.

A Demonstration of Behavior Processes. Appleton-Century-Crofts, color, 28 min.
Skinner discusses and demonstrates behavioral control.

Miracle of the Mind. CBS, b/w, 27 min. Reviews brain functions, electrical and chemical stimulation, effect of drugs on intellectual performance and motivation.
Discusses RNA and McConnell's research in memory transfer. Speculates about
"smart pills."

Human Memory. Harcourt, Brace, Jovanovich, color, 28 min. Gordon Bower demonstrates short-term and long-term memory, memory aids, and cognitive distortions
attending reconstruction of memory.

Information Processing. McGraw-Hill/CRM, color 28 min. David Steinberg and psychologist Donald Norman use a coctail party to demonstrate how people receive, store, and retrieve information.

Short-Term Visual Memory. Bell Labs, b/w, 18 min. Shows research findings on short-term visual memory.

The Power of Positive Reinforcement. McGraw-Hill/CRM, color, 28 min. Demonstrates application of behavior modification principles to enhance worker productivity and job satisfaction.

The Skinner Revolution: Close-up of a Great Thinker and His Influential Ideas. The Media Guild, color, 22 min. Contains descriptive material on operant conditioning and philosophical discussion.

Reward and Punishment. CRM/McGraw-Hill, color, 14 min. Applies reward and punishment to shaping the behavior of children. Discusses controversies concerning punishment.

Self-Management of Behavior. The Media Guild, color, 33 min. Applies principles of learning to teach children to regulate their own behavior.

Memory. CRM/McGraw-Hill, color, 30 min. Excellent 1980 discussion of memory and factors in remembering and forgetting.

Problem-Solving Strategies: The Syntectics Approach. CRM/McGraw-Hill, color, 27 min. Demonstrates how problems are solved at Syntectics Inc.

Creative Problem Solving. CRM/McGraw-Hill, color, 28 min. A 1980 introduction to psychodynamic and physiological theories of creativity. Shows group problem solving by professionals.

Chapter 5: Motivation and Emotion

Human Aggression: Key to Survival. NET, b/w, 28 min. Presents ethological views of Konrad Lorenz. Lorenz offers his views concerning control of aggressive "instincts" in people. An ethological approach.

But First This Message. Action for Children's Television, color. 15 min. Shows excerpts from TV shows and commercials, children's reactions, and comments of concerned professionals.

The Need to Achieve. NET Focus on Behavior Series, b/w, 28 min. David McClelland traces the development of the concept of achievement motivation, including use of projective testing.

The Fat Fighters. Brigham Young University, color, 21 min. Follows eight overweight women in a reducing program. Demonstrates role of motivational variables such as social attitudes, "will power," hunger, and so on.

What Happens in Emotion? Indiana University, color, 30 min. Describes physiological determinants of emotion, including sympathetic and parasympathetic arousal, discusses the reflex and emergency theories of emotion, and explores facial expres-sion of emotions.

Human Aggression. Harper & Row Media, color 32 min. Depicts aggression in real life
and relates aggression to scientific principles and empirical findings.

The Psychology of Eating. Harcourt, Brace, Jovanovich, color, 29 min. A fine film that
explores the causes of eating in people and lower animals. Experimental evidence
ranging from the roles of the hypothalamus to those of external cues is presented.

A New Look at Motivation. CRM/McGraw-Hill, color, 32 min. A good 1980 film of
David McClelland discussing social motives including the needs for power,
achieve-ment, affiliation, and approval.

Chapter 6: Developmental Psychology

Development. McGraw-Hill/CRM, color, 33 min. Broadly samples methods in developmental psychology, and introduces viewer to psychologists working in this area.

Prenatal Development. McGraw-Hill/CRM, color 23 min. Traces prenatal development
from conception through embryonic stage. Shows development and functions of
umbilical cord and placenta, and organ systems.

Sex-Role Development. McGraw-Hill/CRM, color, 23 min. Examines the influence of
sex role stereotypes on many areas of life.

Growing Up Female: As Six Become One. New Day Films, color, 50 min. Focuses on
the socialization processes that influence six women and girls, aged four to thirty-
five.

Men's Lives. New Day Films, color 43 min. Focuses on social forces that influence the
development of male self-concept and image in America.

Rock-A-Bye Baby. Time-Life Films, color, 28 min. Explores research in effects of
social deprivation, emphasizing research of Spitz and Bowlby.

Tim: His Sensory-Motor Development. University of California Instructional Media
Library, color 32 min. Follows sensorimotor development of a normal male infant
from seven to twenty-two months. Illustrates concepts of Jean Piaget.

The Precious Years. Xerox Films, color 25 min. Documents children's programs that
attempt to enhance development according to the developmental schemes of
Piaget and Erikson.

Imprinting. Appleton-Century Crofts, color, 38 min. Demonstrates how and when
imprinting occurs in duck, chicks, and other birds by showing experiments.

Childhood: The Enchanted Years. Ronox, color, 55 min. An MGM documentary on the
work of Piaget, Bruner, Postman, and others.

Mother Love. CBS Carousel, color 21 min. Classical presentation in which Harry Harlow demonstrates his use of wire and terry cloth surrogate mothers to explore
attachment in infant monkeys.

Infancy. Harper & Row Media, color 21 min. Illustrates infant development of object permanence, stranger anxiety, separation anxiety, visual–motor coordination, and so forth.

Cognition. Harper & Row Media, color, 31 min. Illustrates Piaget's stages of cognitive development from sensorimotor through formal operational functioning.

A Cross–Cultural Approach to Cognition. Harper & Row Media, color, 22 min. Demonstrates that an invariant sequence of developmental milestones in cognitive development occurs across cultures.

Invention of the Adolescent. National Film Board of Canada, b/w, 28 min. Historical presentation suggests that adolescence is a product of the Industrial Revolution that meets society's economic needs by keeping youth off the job market for several years, thus contributing to adolescent frustration and a generation gap.

Adolesence: The Winds of Change. Harper & Row Media, color, 30 min. Sexual, physical, and cognitive changes of adolescence are discussed by Conger, Elkind, Kaga, and a number of adolescents.

The Conscience of a Child. NET Focus on Behavior series, b/w, 27 min. Excellent presentation by Robert Sears of research into factors leading to development of conscience in children.

Weekend. Mass Media Associates, color, 12 min. Yugoslavian film shows how elderly persons are cared for yet ignored.

Cognitive Development. McGraw–Hill/CRM, color, 20 min. Contrasts Piaget's stage approach to cognitive development with the behavioral approach. Piaget receives somewhat preferential treatment.

Aging. McGraw–Hill/CRM, color, 22 min. Depicts process of aging.

Development of the Adult. Association Films, color, 25 min. Shows that adulthood, as childhood, has a number of "stages" that persons go through.

Prenatal Development. McGraw–Hill/CRM, color 23 min. Excellent account of effect of endogenous and exogenous substances on fetal development.

Imprinting. Pennslyvania State University, color, 37 min. A good review of imprinting in several species.

Dr. Jean Piaget with Dr. Barbel Inhelder: Parts 1 and 2. Pennsylvania State University, color, 40 min. each. A 1969 interview.

Physical Development. McGraw–Hill/CRM, color, 21 min. A 1978 overview of physical development emphasizing perceptual and motor skills through adolesence.

Chapter 7: Personality

Individual Differences. McGraw–Hill/CRM, color, 18 min. Explores individual differences, and the broad range of normal personality traits.

Personality: Early Childhood, Middle Childhood; Adolesence. McGraw–Hill/CRM, color, 20 min. each. Explorations of personality at three stages of childhood.

Personality. McGraw—Hill/CRM, color, 33 min. Profiles the personality of a male
        college student concerned about his masculinity.

Freud: The Hidden Nature of Man. Indiana University, color, 29 min. Explores Freud's
        psychoanalytic theory: Freud's personal background, psychic structures, Oedipus
        complex, dream analysis, and so forth.

Dr. Ernest Jones. NBC TV, b/w, 28 min. A film of the 1950s in which Freud's biog-
        rapher reminisces about Freud and outlines basic psychoanaytic concepts.

The Story of Carl Gustav Jung: In Search of Soul; 67,000 Dreams; The Mystery that
        Heals. Time—Life Films, b/w, about 30 min. each. Well—done comprehensive
        survey of Jung's concepts, his relationship and break with Sigmund Freud, his view
        of the collective unconscious. Shows Jung travelling around the world col—lecting
        evidence about universal "archetypes."

Ratman. Time—Life Films, color, 53 min. Dramatizes Freud's analysis of an obsessive
        patient dubbed "Ratman" by Freud. Fine illustration of Freud's search for deep-
        seated causes of rage, anger, and guilt.

Dr. Gordon Allport, Parts 1 and 2. Pennsylvania State University, b/w, 50 min. each.
        Films produced in 1966 in which Allport presents his views on personality.

Dr. Henry Murray: Part 1. Pennsylvania State University, b/w, 50 min. A 1966 film in
        which Henry Murray presents his views on personality.

Dr. Carl Gustav Jung. Pennsylvania State University, b/w, 38 min. A 1967 interview
        with Jung——one of the last——in which Jung discusses his differences with Freud
        and presents his own views.

Dr. B. F. Skinner, Part I. Pennsylvania State University, b/w, 50 min. A 1966 film in
        which Skinner evaluates Freud's theory of personality and presents his own views.

Dr. Carl Rogers, Part I. Pennsylvania State University, color, 50 min. A 1969 film in
        which Rogers presents his views on people and personality.

Being Abraham Maslow. Pennsylvania State University, b/w, 30 min. A 1972 film in
        which Maslow presents his views on personality.

Sex for Sale. McGraw—Hill/CRM, color 45 min. Includes four vignettes: commercial
        sex in urban centers, the pornography boom, a Detroit neighborhood's battle
        against prostitution, and the life of a street prostitute: Somewhat moralistic
        tone.

The New Sexuality. Films, Inc., color, 26 min. Interviews many persons concerning
        changing or deviant sexual behaviors and moral standards: includes Marilyn
        Cham—bers discussing her pornographic films, an author on bisexuality, a minister
        and his wife, and persons discussing homosexuality, nude encounter groups,
        nonmono—gamous marriages, and so on.

The Sexes: Roles. Filmmakers Library, color 28 min.

The Sexes: What's The Difference? Filmmaker's Library, color, 28 min. Noted
	psycholo—gists like Maccoby, Bardwick, and Horner discuss sex differences and the
	acqui—sition of sex roles.

Women in Management. McGraw—Hill/CRM, color, 29 min. Presents stereotypes of
	women as managers. Depicts responses by men and women in spontaneous discus-
	sion groups.

Pomeroy Takes a Sex History. Multi Media (1525 Franklin Street., San Francisco, CA
	94109), color, 35 min. Shows Dr. Wardell Pomeroy of the Kinsey Institute at
	Indiana University interviewing to obtain a sexual history.

Sex—Role Development. McGraw—Hill/CRM, color, 23 min. Explores ways of decreasing
	sex—role stereotyping among young people.

Homosexuality. McGraw—Hill/CRM, color, 10 min. Two boys react to their belief that
	a friend is homosexual,

A Woman's Place Is in the House. Texture Films (1600 Broadway, New York NY 10019),
	color, 30 min. Elaine Nobel, lesbian leader of the Massachusetts House of Repre-
	sentatives, discusses her homosexuality.

Dirty Business. Multi Media, color 25 min. Interviews with people involved in porno-
	graphy—-actors, producers, attorneys, and the audience.

   Chapter 8: Abnormal Behavior

Neurotic Behavior. McGraw—Hill/CRM, color, 20 min. Illustrates defense mechanisms
	and varieties of neurotic behaviors through the life of a college student, Peter.

Abnormal Behavior: A Mental Hospital. McGraw—Hill/CRM, color, 28 min. Illustrates
	psychotic disorders through a visit to a mental hospital.

Depression. McGraw—Hill/CRM, color, 27 min. Shows a young teacher—housewife ex-
	periencing a depressive episode: shows hospitalization, therapy, eventual
	discharge. Considered by some a depressing film.

Obsessive—Compulsive Neurosis. McGraw—Hill/CRM, color, 30 min. Illustrates exam-
	ples of obsessive—compulsive behavior.

Otto: A Study in Abnormal Psychology: Parts 1—5. Indiana University, color, 25—28 min.
	each. The series of films chronicles pressures on Otto, the development of
	psychopathology, and its treatment from four perspectives: Part 2, Behavioral;
	Part 3, Phenomenological; Part 4, Psychoanalytic; Part 5, Social.

R.D. Laing: A Dialogue on Mental Illness and Its Treatment. Pennsylvania State
	University, color, 21 min. A 1976 film in which Laing presents his sociocultural
	perspective.

One Man's Madness. Pennslyvania State University, color, 32 min. BBC production of
	the development of bipolar disorder in a successful writer. Candid hospital
	scenes.

An Easy Pill to Swallow. McGraw–Hill/CRM, color, 28 min. Discusses anxiety and drug
          addiction, and shows the perils of treating anxiety with drugs.

Alcoholism: A Model of Drug Dependency. Pennsylvania State University, color, 20
          min. Discusses effects of chronic alcoholism, and concepts of addiction, tole-
          rance, and withdrawal.

An Ounce of Prevention. Association Films, inc., color, 26 min. Explores damage done
          by excessive drinking.

US. Churchill Films, color, 28 min. Views substance abuse from a cultural context:
          housewives using tranquilizers and diet pills, businessmen drinking excessively,
          and marijuana use among youth.

Sexual Communication. Washington State University, color, 55 min. Depicts a physi-
          cian/patient interview and provides information concerning psychological and
          physiological factors in sexual relationships. Considered human and humerous.

     Chapter 9: Personality: Theory and Measurement:
     Psychological Assessment of Personality and Intelligence

Individual Differences. McGraw–Hill/CRM, color, 18 min. Explores individual differ-
          ences, and the broad range of normal personality traits.

Personality: Early Childhood; Middle Childhood; Adolescence. McGraw–Hill/CRM,
          color, 20 min. each. Explorations of personality at three stages of childhood.

Personality. McGraw–Hill/CRM, color, 33 min. Profiles the personality of a male
          college student concerned about his masculinity.

Freud: The Hidden Nature of Man. Indiana University, color, 29 min. Explores Freud's
          psychoanalytic theory: Freud's personal background, psychic structures, Oedipus
          complex, dream analysis, and so forth.

Dr. Ernest Jones. NBC TV, b/w, 28 min. A film of the 1950s in which Freud's biogra-
          pher reminisces about Freud and outlines basic psychoanalytic concepts.

The Story of Carl Gustav Jung: In Search of Soul; 67,000 Dreams; The Mystery That
          Heals. Time–Life Films, b/w, about 30 min. each. Well–done comprehensive
          survey of Jung's concepts, his relationship and break with Sigmund Freud, his view
          of the collective unconscious. Shows Jung traveling around the world collecting
          evidence about universal "archetypes."

Ratman. Time–Life Films, color, 53 min. Dramatizes Freud's analysis of an obsessive
          patient dubbed "Ratman" by Freud. Fine illustration of Freud's search for deep-
          seated causes of rage, anger, and guilt.

Dr. Gordon Allport, Parts 1 and 2. Pennslyvania State University, b/w/, 50 min. each.
          Films produced in 1966 in which Allport presents his views on personality.

Dr. Raymond Cattell, Parts 1 and 2. Pennsylvania State University, b/w, 50 min. each.
          Films produced in 1966 which presents Cattell's views on personality and discuss
          the development of tests like the 16PF.

Dr. Henry Murray: Part 1. Pennsylvania State University, b/w, 50 min. A 1966 film in which Henry Murray presents his views on personality.

Dr. Carl Gustav Jung. Pennsylvania State University, b/w, 38 min. A 1967 interview with Jung—one of the last—in which Jung discusses his differences with Freud and presents his own views.

Dr. B.F. Skinner, Part 1. Pennsylvania State University, b/w, 50 min. A 1966 film in which Skinner evaluates Freud's theory of personality and presents his own views.

Dr. Carl Rogers, Part I. Pennsylvania State University, color, 50 min. A 1969 film in which Rogers presents his views on people and personality.

Being Abraham Maslow. Pennsylvania State University, b/w, 30 min. A 1972 film in which Maslow presents his views on personality.

Creative Problem Solving. CRM/McGraw-Hill, color, 28 min. A 1980 introduction to psychodynamic and physiological theories of creativity. Shows group problem solving by professionals.

Intelligence: A Complex Concept. CRM/McGraw-Hill, color, 28 min. This 1978 film illustrates definitions of intelligence and methods of, and controversies about, intelligence testing.

I.Q. Myth: Parts 1 and 2. Pennsylvania State University, color, 50 min. A 1975 production by CBS news which generally takes the stand that intelligence tests are culturally biased.

CBS Reports: The IQ Myth. CBS News and Carousel Films, color, 50 min. Scathing critique of concept of IQ and of intelligence testing by Dan Rather. Many psychologists consider film negatively biased.

Chapter 10: Psychotherapy

Titticut Follies. Zipporah, b/w, 90 min. Highly controversial film depicts Bridgewater State Hospital in Massachusetts. Rated R.

Behavior Therapy or Client-Centered Therapy? Whitely Distinguished Contributions to Counseling Series, b/w, 30 min. Debates the two forms of therapy, presenting behavior therapy as rigorous but controlling, and client-centered therapy as philosophically attractive but scientifically muddied.

Games People Play: The Theory; The Practice. NET, b/w, 30 min. each. Interviews Eric Berne, who originated transactional analysis. In the first film he traces development of TA, and outlines some games. In the second film he defines terms like Child, Parent, and Adult ego states, game, and script.

Behavior Therapy: An Introduction. Association Films, color. 23 min. Depicts use of behavior therapy to help a woman control her child's temper tantrums, a college student reduce speech anxiety, and a young man establish social contacts with women.

Madness and Medicine. McGraw–Hill/CRM, color, 45 min. Investigates use of chemotherapy, electroconvulsive therapy and psychosurgery in mental institutions.
Graphic and useful.

Therapy: What Do You Want Me to Say? McGraw–Hill/CRM, color, 15 min. Provides
information about use of psychotherapy.

R.D. Laing: A Dialogue on Mental Illness and Its Treatment. Association Films, color,
22 min. Illustrates the controversial sociocultural theroists' theoretical approach
and treatment of abnormal behavior.

Psychotherapy. McGraw–Hill/CRM, color, 26 min. Excellent presentation of reasons
for seeking therapy and of therapist variables that contribute to successful therapy.

Fragile Mind. Pennsylvania State University, color, 52 min. A 1973 ABC documentary
that shows why people seek therapy and various therapeutic approaches.

Psychoanalysis. Indiana University, b/w, 30 min. Two psychoanalysts discuss a case.

Psychotheraphy in Progress: The Case of Miss Mun. Pennslyvania State University,
b/w, 56 min. An old (1955) film of a therapy session with Carl Rogers. Authentic
client-centered therapy.

One Step at a Time: An Introduction to Behavioral Modification. Pennslyvania State
University, color, 28 min. Illustrates behavioral charting and uses of reinforcement. A decent introductory film, 1973 vintage.

Behavior Therapy Demonstration. Pennslyvania State University, color, 32 min., Dr.
Joseph Wolpe demonstrates his technique of systematic desensitization to treat
anxiety.

Actualization Through Assertion. Media Guild, color, 28 min. Illustrates many techniques of assertiveness training well.

Awareness. Pennslyvania State University, color, 29 min. A 1969 film in which Fritz
Perls leads a Gestalt therapy group.

Chapter 11: Social Psychology

The Social Animal. NET Focus on Behavior Series, b/w, 27 min. A number of psychologists reenact classic experiments: Asch, Sherif, Festinger, and Deutsch. Of
historical interest.

Communication: The Nonverbal Agenda. McGraw–Hill/CRM, color, 30 min. Illustrates
body language in an organizational setting.

Cross–Cultural Development of Sex roles and Social Standards. Harper & Row Media,
color, 25 min. Depicts acquisition of sex roles in Guatemala, Japan, and Kenya.

Invitation to Social Psychology. Harper & Row Media, color, 25 min. Stanley Milgram
narrates. Depicts studies on social influence, including obedience to authority,
bystander effect, and simulated prison. Fine film.

Prejudice: Causes, Consequences, Cures. McGraw-Hill, CRM, color, 24 min. Depicts research findings on prejudice against women and minorities, perpetuation of stereotypes in the media, methods for promoting cooperation in newly integrated classrooms, and reeducation of discrimination through legal means.

Nonverbal Communication, Harper & Row Media, color, 22 min. Examines research findings on gestures, bodily posture, tone of voice, eye contact, and facial expression.

Conformity and Independence. Harper & Row media, color, 23 min. Stanley Milgram narrates findings on norm formation, group pressure, compliance, conformity, and so on.

Obedience. University of Iowa, b/w, 50 min. Depicts Milgram's classic experiments on obedience to authority. Subjects explain why they shocked confederate of experimenter or why they chose not to.

When Will People Help? The Social Psychology of Bystander Intervention. Harcourt Brayce Jovanovich, color, 25 min. Daryl Bem narrates theory and research findings (Latane and Darley) on the bystander effect.

Social Psychology. Pennslyvania State University, color, 33 min. Film is partly introductory, focuses on social comparison theory, attitudes, and the formation of prejudice.

Eye of the Storm. Pennslyvania State University, color, 29 min. Chronicles an elementary-school experiment on prejudice in which children are told that intelligence is based on eye color.

Group Dynamics: Groupthink. Pennslyvania State University, color, 23 min. Irving Janis discusses the group decision-making process involved in historical events such as Pearl Harbor and the Bay of Pigs invasion.

CHAPTER 1

WHAT IS PSYCHOLOGY?

LEARNING OBJECTIVES

After reading this chapter the student should be able to:

1. Define psychology and discuss the controversy concerning its definition.
2. Define and contrast the terms "observable behaviors" and "mental processes."
3. List and discuss the goals of psychology.
4. Explain the difference between pure research and applied research.
5. Explain the differences among the many types of psychologists involved in clinical services, research, and industry. (For example: What is the difference between a clinical psychologist and a counseling psychologist?)
6. Indicate the fields in which large numbers of psychologists specialize, and the places in which large numbers of psychologists work.

7. Compare and contrast the four major theoretical perspectives in psychology: biological, cognitive, psychoanalytic, and behavioral.
8. Explain how each of these perspectives accounts for human aggression.
9. Trace the historical development of the cognitive perspective.
10. Trace the historical development of the behavioral perspective.
11. Define naturalistic observation and discuss its uses and limitations.
12. Define and explain the major features of the experimental method. (For example: What is a double-blind study?)
13. Explain the survey method.
14. Discuss the significance of the LITERARY DIGEST survey.
15. Discuss the case study method, its uses and limitations.
16. Discuss the correlational method, comparing and contrasting it to the experimental method.
17. Discuss ethical issues in psychology, including confidentiality, informed consent, and the use of deception in research.

LECTURE NOTES

Lecture: Psychologists in Different Specialties

I: General Comments
   A. Psychologists in any specialty may engage in research and/or teaching. Most psychologists (57 percent) are employed by colleges and universities.

II: Psychologists in Clinical Services
   A. Clinical Psychologists: Most common specialty (36 percent), diagnose abnormal behaviors, psychotheraphy.
   B. Counseling Psychologists: Help clients with adjustment (academic, vocational, interpersonal) problems, use psychological tests.
   C. School Psychologists: Use tests to place students, help students adjust to learning environment, consult.
   D. Educational Psychologists: May construct standardized tests (item analysis, reliability, validity), consult about curricula, learning environments.
   E. Community Psychologists: Often do clinical work in CMHCs, may consult with community to prevent mental illness.

III: Psychologists in Research
   A. Developmental Psychologists: Study children to promote healthy development, may study later ages and stages for same purpose.
   B. Personality Psychologists: Formulate and examine theories of personality (how individuals adapt to their situations).
   C. Social Psychologists: Study how people perceive and influence each other (social perception, persuasion, obedience, conformity).
   D. Environmental Psychologists: Study people in their physical environment; effects of pollution, crowding, ambient temperature, and so on.
   E. Experimental Psychologists: Study basic processes of learning, motivation, physiology, and so forth.

IV: Psychologists in Industry
   A. Industrial Psychologists: Study ways to improve worker productivity and job satisfaction (for example, music in factories? Color of walls? Placement of machines?)

B. Consumer Psychologists: Study factors influencing consumer behavior, effective commercials, and ads, placement of products in supermarkets, and so forth.

DISCUSSION QUESTIONS

1. What is psychology? The purpose of this question is to dispel the lay equation of psychology with clinical psychology, and with Freudian psychology. Ask students what they had thought psychology was at the time when they signed up to take the course. It can also be useful to compare students' image of the psychiatrist, the social worker and the counselor.

2. What do psychologists mean by controlling behavior as one of their goals? Here I squarely face the fact that this is both a controversial and troublesome issue. Some psychologists mean that they attempt to control the behavior of animals, some that they attempt to help people take control of their own lives. On the other hand, psychologists do study the determinants of behavior, and, in their experiments, they manipulate the hypothesized determinants of behavior in order to study the effects of such manipulations. If time permits, I may digress into a discussion of the controversy surrounding behavior modification--but this may be delayed for discussion in Chapter 10 as well.

3. The following question indirectly promotes understanding of the nature of psychology as a science: "What do psychologists of different specialties have in common?" Answers include the psychologist's scientific approach to the explanation, prediction, and control of behavior. An inferior but current answer is that all psychologists may teach, or conduct research.

4. I present the following anecdote to promote understanding of the necessity for the control group in experimentation: "An experimental psychologist wished to determine the effects of a new drug on rats. On Friday afternoon the rats in the laboratory were injected with the substance and returned to their cages. A lab assistant left a lab window open for the weekend, which was bitterly cold. On Monday morning the lab assistant, who was first to arrive, found all the rats frozen to death. He shut the window quickly so his error would not be discovered. Later that morning the psychologist concluded that the new drug had killed the rats. Could precautions have been taken so that this incorrect inference would not have been drawn?"
    Indicate that use of a control gorup would have resulted in the (unfortunate) deaths of control rats as well, and the incorrect conclusion would have been avoided.

5. Draw students out on their views as to whether the Lang study on alcohol and aggression, which involved deception of subjects, was ethical. Why or why not? Is it possible to mention other laboratory procedures and ask students for their thoughts on whether they are ethical. A handful:

    The Masters and Johnson laboratory observations of sexual behavior.
    The Milgram studies on obedience to authority.
    The Harlow studies on social deprivation in infant monkeys.
    The "sacrifice" of laboratory animals.

The purpose of this exercise is not to arrive at stock simplistic answers, but to encourage students to comprehend some of the dilemmas facing psychologists as they attempt to advance the state of psychological knowledge.

MATERIALS FOR STUDENT DISTRIBUTION

Handout 1.1: Love Story

This TIME magazine (January 2, 1978) article illustrates many errors that people make in observing behavior, especially in animals, and in attribution of cause and effect. First it shows the error of anthropomorphization--attributing human emotions such as short-temperedness, balefulness, and love to animals. Also, the story attributes changes in the animals' behavior to loss of the human audience, just as people claim that their pets "miss" them when they are away. It is just as possible that the changes in behavior may be attributed to disturbances brought about by the renovation process-construction noise, and the like. And it is also possible that the observations of behavior change are unreliable; there is no evidence of a systematic attempt to measure and document them.

News items presented in these handouts may be abbreviated versions of the originals, but they have not been otherwise altered. Thus it is advised that instructors read them carefully to determine whether certain statements are scientifically unsound and should thus receive commentary in the classroom.

Handout 1.2: Cutting Out Monkey Business

This rather sensationalistic article from TIME magazine (February 6, 1978) nonetheless highlights some of the ethical dilemmas psychologists and other scientists face when they undertake research with infrahuman species. Morarji Desai, is no longer Prime Minister of India. Still, the types of questions that concerned him remain current.

Handout 1.3: The Psychological Viewpoint Questionnaire

This questionnaire may be administered to accompany Chapter 1 or Chapter 7 (Personality). Developed by psychologist William R. Miller of the University of New Mexico, it indicates whether respondents are in sympathy with a behavioral (B), existential (E), humanistic (H), or psychoanalytic (P) point of view. Chapter 1 of the text does not discuss the existential point of view, so students will be in need of some elaboration.

Handout 1.4: Scoring the Psychological Viewpoint Questionnaire

This score key accompanies handout 1.3. Students simply add up the number of points they earn in each column to determine the view of human nature with which their responses suggest greater sympathy. It may be interesting to publicly interview students who earn extremely high scores on a particular scale.

CHAPTER 2

BIOLOGY AND BEHAVIOR

LEARNING OBJECTIVES

After reading this chapter the student should be able to

1. List and define the parts of the neuron.
2. Explain the difference between afferent and efferent neurons.
3. Discuss research concerning whether we lose brain cells as we grow older.
4. Explain the electrochemical process by which neural impulses travel.
5. Explain the "all-or-none" principle of neural transmission.
6. Explain the functions of different kinds of synapses and neurotransmitters.
7. Explain what is meant by a nerve.
8. Diagram the various divisions of the nervous system.
9. Explain how spinal reflexes work.
10. List and locate the major structures of the hindbrain, midbrain, forebrain (see the first exercise, below).
11. Explain the known functions of the parts of the brain.
12. Summarize the activities of the sympathetic and parasympathetic branches of the autonomic nervous system.
13. Locate the four lobes of each hemisphere of the cerebral cortex and explain the functions of various sections of these lobes.
14. Summarize the findings of divided-brain research.
15. Summarize research findings on electrical stimulation of the brain (ESB).
16. Explain the functions of the major hormones secreted by the pituitary gland, the pancreas, the thyroid and adrenal glands, the testes and the ovaries.
17. Explain glandular disorders like hyperglycemia and hyperthyroidism.
18. Explain what psychologists mean by "nature" and "nurture."
19. Define genes and chromosomes, and describe human chromosomal structure.
20. Differentiate between dominant and recessive traits.
21. Differentiate between monozygotic and dizygotic twins.
22. Explain what is meant by genetic abnormalities like Down's Syndrome and phenyl-ketonuria (PKU).
23. Summarize the results of experiments in selective breeding.
24. Explain the technique of amniocentesis.

LECTURE NOTES

Lecture: Finding Your Way Around the Human Brain

　　　I usually begin this lecture with some self-deprecatory remark about my artwork never winning prizes. Then I make some broad, sweeping lines on the blackboard, erase some, modify others by elongation, and try to wind up with a figure that looks something like the one on the left. I label parts as I talk about them. (Label as many parts as you can without cluttering your drawing so that it becomes incomprehensible.) Then I make a comment about regretting erasing my immortal art, erase the parts of the brain, and then draw in the lobes, as at the right. Then I discuss the functions located in each lobe.

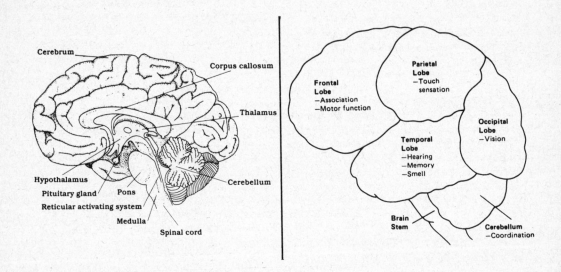

I. The Hindbrain

　　A.　Medulla: Heartbeat, respiration.
　　B.　Pons ("bridge" in Latin): Respiration, transmission of information concerning bodily movement between cerebellum and cerebrum.
　　C.　Cerebellum ("little brain" in Latin): Control of motor behavior, maintenance of balance; injury leads to stumbling loss of muscle tone, and so on.

II. The Midbrain

　　A.　The Reticular Activating System (RAS): Attention, arousal, sleep; electrical stimulation awakens; injury may lead to coma.

III. The Forebrain

　　A.　Thalamus: Relay of sensory information to cortex (arrow from eyes, then to occipital lobe); involved in attention, sleep.
　　B.　Hypothalamus (tiny yet involved in motivation, emotion, and so forth) temperature, hunger thirst, sex, aggression.

36

C. Basal Ganglia: Coordination (deterioration leads to Parkinson's disease.
D. Limbic system: Memory, eating, sex, aggression.
E. Cerebrum: Sensation, motor control, thought, and language. Cerebrum sets people apart from other animals. Four lobes of cerebral cortex.

DISCUSSION QUESTIONS

1. Where is research on biology and behavior leading? What might happen if scientists discovered the function of every part of the brain? Why?

2. Imagine a situation in which a psychologist attempts to market a device that permits people to electrically stimulate a certain part of the brain and experience waves of pleasure that are more intense, say, than the pleasures of orgasm or even (I usually fill in the name of a particularly luscious local brand of ice cream or pizza or taco). People who acquire these devices stimulate their brains for hours on end and lose all interest in work, family, national problems, and so forth. The government begins hearings to arrive at a decision as to whether legislation banning the devices ought to be sought. What would you say if you were called to testify?

3. The following discussion question helps students understand whether they place more value on their sense of self-importance, or the possible "improvement" of the human species, and to identify human traits that they believe have value:
    "A psychologist demonstrates that through selective breeding with human beings it is possible to create people with levels of intelligence far exceeding the average. (With the recent establishment of at least one sperm bank intended to propagate the very brilliant, this concept is not necessarily far off the mark.) A number of people call for legislation preventing the reproduction of inferior individuals, and requiring that potential parents receive psychological tests, as a result of which they may be given permits to reproduce. The government undertakes hearings before passing any legislation. What would you say if you were called to testify."
    Watch out! This topic generates heated discussions. A number of issues that are likely to be raised include the following: Do people have an inalienable right to reproduce whenever and with whomever they wish? Should intelligence be the major criterion for reproduction permits? What would the cutoff scores be and who would determine them? Would my own level of ability eventually be viewed as substandard? Is there such a thing as a goal for the human species?
    Once all feelings have been aired, I emphasize the point that all this is hypothetical. As the chapter notes, for example, maze-learning ability in rats, which can be selectively bred, is not the same thing as intelligent behavior in humans. However, with the world population explosion, it is not altogether a fantasy that some societies may be developing criteria for making decisions at some point in our own lifetimes, about who may reproduce. There is already legislation in Australia and the United Kingdom regarding experimentation and destruction of stored gametes. You could ask students to try to envision a world where sex and reproduction have been separated from one another.

4. A related and also heated discussion topic involves some of the science fiction/fantasy questions raised by the prospect of genetic engineering. For example: Would it be ethical for scientists to create a BRAVE NEW WORLD class of dull individuals to carry out menial tasks for society? What if these persons appeared perfectly "happy" carrying out such tasks? Would it be proper to create superhumans-- extremely intelligent and creative individuals?

Such issues have a frightening ring to them, and are reminiscent of Hitler's Germany. I personally find it difficult to consider them. On the other hand, many students think about these issues when they read about topics such as selective breeding and genetic engineering. Just recently the Supreme Court ruled that individuals could own patents to new forms of life produced in the laboratory! These issues are current and they will be bantered about. I guess I would rather have them discussed in my classroom, where I can point out that certain views may be contradictory to Western values, or are simply illogical.

At some point I emphasize my belief that there is no such thing as bad knowledge--only the possible improper application of knowledge. Occasionally I recount the dilemma of the scientists who participated in the development of the atom bomb.

MATERIALS FOR STUDENT DISTRIBUTION

Handout 2.1: Some Dominant and Recessive Traits

This is a chart listing dominant versus recessive traits.

Handout 2.2: Coping with Eve's Curse

This is a news item from TIME magazine (July 27, 1981). News items present in these handouts may be abbreviated versions of the originals, but they have not been otherwise altered. Thus it is advised that instructors read them carefully to determine whether certain statements are scientifically unsound and should thus receive commentary in the classroom.

Handout 2.3: The Making of a Mighty Mouse

Genetic transplants from NEWSWEEK, (December 27, 1982).

CHAPTER 3

SENSATION AND PERCEPTION

LEARNING OBJECTIVES

After reading this chapter the student should be able to:

1. Define and contrast the terms sensation and perception.
2. Explain the structure of light, including the frequency and amplitude of light waves.
3. Define psychophysics and explain the historical contribution of Ernst Weber.
4. Define absolute and difference thresholds for an energy source.
5. List and locate the parts of the eye.
6. Explain the functions of the parts of the eye.
7. Explain how rods and cones differ in dark adaptation.
8. Define nearsightedness, farsightedness, and presbyopia.
9. Explain and contrast the trichromatic and opponent-process theories of color vision.

10. Define monochromat, dichromat, and trichromat.
11. List and explain the monocular and binocular cues for depth perception discussed in the text.
12. Explain size constancy, shape constancy, and color constancy.
13. List and explain the Gestalt rules for perceptual organization that are discussed in the text.
14. Explain the effects of visual illusions by using the rules of perceptual constancy.
15. Explain the perception of actual movement and of illusions of movement.
16. Explain the structure of sound waves, including pitch and loudness.
17. List and locate the parts of the ear.
18. Explain the functions of the parts of the ear.
19. Explain and differentiate between the place and frequency theories of perceiving the pitch of a sound.
20. Explain the nature of odor. (What is an "odor"?)
21. Discuss research concerning the possible role of phermomones in human sexual behavior.
22. List the four basic tastes.
23. Differentiate between taste cells and taste buds.
24. List four kinds of skin sensations.
25. Explain the possible functioning of acupuncture through the gate theory of pain or the release of endorphins.
26. Define kinesthesis and vestibular sense.
27. List the four stages of NREM sleep and the features of each.
28. Describe REM sleep.
29. Summarize research concerning the functions of sleep, focusing on the effects of sleep deprivation and on long vs. short sleepers.
30. Discuss dreams, including theories of their content, and distinguish between nightmares and night terrors.
31. Describe the psychological correlates of insomnia.
32. Explain the rationales for psychological methods for overcoming insomnia.
33. Discuss narcolepsy, apnea, and the deep-sleep disorders.

LECTURE NOTES

Lecture: The Human Eye

Draw a figure of the human eye on the blackboard. If you show an image projected onto the retina, it is a simple matter to make it a stick figure.

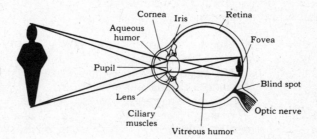

I. Comparison of Eye to Camera

   A. Only certain amount of light allowed into both if images are to be clear.
   B. Image projected upside down onto retina and onto photosensitive plate.
   C. Lens focuses image in both.

II.   Parts of the Eye

    A.   Cornea (from Latin for "horn," suggesting hardness): Light passes through here first; may digress into cornea transplants.
    B.   Pupil: Adjustment to light source is reflex.
    C.   Lens: Focuses light; becomes brittle with age, leading to condition called presbyopia.
    D.   Retina: Like the film of a camera; contains many types of cells.
        1.   About 100 million rods, sensitive to light-dark only; absent at fovea, thickest toward lens.
        2.   About 6 million cones, sensitive to color; sparse near lens; fovea contains cones only. Can compare dark adaptation of cones and rods.
        3.   Ganglion cells: Outermost layer of retina; axons form optic nerve, which conducts visual input to thalamus, from where it is conducted to and projected in the occipital lobe.
        4.   Bipolar cells: Conduct messages from rods and cones to ganglion cells.
        5.   Fovea: Most sensitive part of the eye.
        6.   Blind spot: Spot where optic nerve conducts visual sensory input from the eye.

DISCUSSION QUESTIONS

1.   What would it be like not to be able to experience pain? I usually mention that pain serves as a warning device that something is wrong and thus probably requires attention. I list some diseases for which pain is a symptom, and include muscle pains as a sign that one should temporarily discontinue exercising or working. Students are fascinated to learn that a few rare individuals apparently do not experience pain.

2.   Film and television scenes are two-dimensional. Yet viewers perceive events to occur in three dimensions. How do viewers perceive depth on such a two-dimensional surface? This question calls for a recital of monocular cures for depth.

3.   Is it fair for the armed services to restrict flight training to individuals who have adequate uncorrected visual acuity? Couldn't a person with glasses or contact lenses pilot an aircraft?

4.   Consider the philosophical issue: "A tree falls in the forest. No one is around to hear it. Does it make a sound?"
    I point out that we must consider the meaning of the concept "sound." If by sound we mean the alternate expansion and compression of air molecules that accompanies the slap of the tree against the ground, the sound is present. Here the sound is an energy source that is capable of stimulating sensory receptors. But if we think of the "sound" as a sensation made possible by this energy source, the sensation would not be present, since sensation results from the stimulation of sensory receptors by an energy source.
    Some wag in the class may point out, "But how do we know that the falling of every tree would cause compression and expansion of air molecules?" The student is referring to Hume's problem of inferrence--that we cannot with certainty know that all instances of a kind would be similar. It is an inferential leap. Hume's answer was that we must live by habit (normal expectation). If I am in a good mood I usually answer, "The best predictor of future behavior is past behavior in a similar situation." If my stomach is growling for lunch I usually say, "Trust, pure trust."

5. Is it possible to program dreams? I mention that dreams largely reflect the residues of the day, and that some have claimed that they can program dreams by controlling what they think about as they fall asleep. Sometimes we also realize that we are having a dream, and, as a result, some of us wake up. Has anyone in the class ever tried to remain in the dream at such a time, and managed to subtly shape the outcome of the dream by having certain events take place?

6. How many class members have had nightmares that they were trying to run away from something, but they just could not get their feet moving properly? Invite them to share their dreams with the class. Have any students dreamed that they showed up late for an important examination, or that they could not locate the room in which the exam was being held? Have any students dreamed that they just completed the exam they were to have the following day? Then they dream that their taking the exam was in fact just a dream--and now they're completing it? Then they dream that their second taking of the exam was just a dream--and now?

MATERIALS FOR STUDENT DISTRIBUTION

Handout 3.1: The Baldwin and Poggendorf Illusions

These illusions are, of course, named after their originators. In showing the Baldwin Illusion, ask the class which of the lines connecting the two boxes looks longer, the upper line or the lower line? Most students will agree that the upper line looks longer although some may say that they can "tell" that they are really the same. In the case of the Baldwin Illusion, the upper line probably looks longer because of the principle of size constancy. That is, if the two sets of boxes were the same size, it would mean that the upper figure must be farther away. If the upper figure is farther away, then a line that appears to be about equal in length must actually be longer.

In showing the Poggendorf Illusion, ask the class whether the diagonal lines intersect. The line on the right appears to be higher than the line on the left (it seems as though it would continue above the line on the left), but a straightedge or ruler will quickly show that the lines do, in fact, intersect or meet. According to Coren and Girgus (Seeing is Deceiving, Hillsdale, NJ: Lawrence Erlbaum Associates, 1978), the illusion can be explained by a combination of physical ("structural") and cognitive ("processing") factors. A structural or physical effect is determined by the biological and optical characteristics of the eye, whereas a processing strategy reflects an active process of perception that is influenced by experience and learning. Coren and Girgus used special optical techniques to estimate that about 40 percent of the Poggendorf Illusion's sources of confusion stem from physical or structural factors, while about another 29 percent stem from the process of perception. The remaining 21 percent is attributed to undetermined structural and/or cognitive factors.

Handout 3.2: The Distorted Room Illusion

The top figure in this handout is a photo of two men looking into the Ames Distorted Room. This photo is rather shocking to many students; they find it difficult to believe that one person can be so much larger than another, who also appears to be an adult. When students are asked which person is larger, they will certainly be thinking that the person on the right is much larger, although I always have a couple of students who are "on to" the fact that some trick is at hand, and either give the opposite response or refuse to play.

In any event, the lower figure shows that the person on the right was actually much closer to the viewer than the person at the left, and that the difference in size

may be attributed to distance. The Ames Distorted Room creates an illusion by con-
founding depth cues: because the person on the right does not appear to be closer (assuming that the viewer perceives the room as being rectangular, as rooms normally
are), he is perceived as being larger.

CHAPTER 4

LEARNING AND COGNITION

LEARNING OBJECTIVES

After reading this chapter the student should be able to:

1. Define learning from behavioral and cognitive perspectives. (That is, as a change
   in behavior vs. an inferred internal process.)
2. Define, describe, and contrast the processes of classical conditioning and operant
   conditioning.
3. Define and explain the roles of the US, CS, UR, and CR in classical conditioning.
4. Define and provide examples of extinction and spontaneous recovery in classical
   conditioning and in operant conditioning.
5. Define and provide examples of generalization and discrimination in classical
   and operant conditioning.
6. Describe the roles of Pavlov, Thorndike, and Skinner in the history of conditioning.
7. Define precisely positive and negative, and primary and secondary reinforcers,
   providing examples of each. (Many students are aggravated by the need for absolute precision in all these definitions, but they are essential to the study of the
   science of psychology.)
8. Differentiate between the concepts of reward and reinforcement, and explain
   why the term reinforcement is more satisfactory to the behaviorist.
9. Explain the disadvantages of using punishment.
10. Explain the various schedules of reinforcement, and explain how to maintain
    behavior indefinitely by using intermittent reinforcement.
11. Describe the process of shaping behaviors.
12. Discuss the controversy concerning the effort to explain all human behavior through
    principles of conditioning.
13. Describe experiments that have led cognitive psychologists to be dissatisfied
    with conditioning as an explanation of all learning.
14. Define insight, latent learning, and observational learning.
15. Define the terms concept and symbol and show how they differ from one another.
16. Explain the following approaches to concept formation: presentation of positive
    and negative instances, verbal explanation, and hypothesis testing.
17. Describe what is meant by the incubation effect.
18. Define the terms functional fixedness and metal set (as applied to problem solv-
    ing), and provide an example of each.

LECTURE NOTES

Lecture: Classical and Operant Conditioning

I. Introductory Remarks

A. Many behaviors believe that human behavior can be explained through principles of classical and operant conditioning.

B. Neither types of learning involves thought, consciousness or a personal effort to learn. They are both automatic and determined fully by environmental or situational factors.

C. In classical conditioning an expectation or association between two stimuli is learned. In operant conditioning an organism learns to "do something" because it is reinforced.

II. Classical Conditioning

A. I begin by describing Pavlov's experiments with meat powder and bells.

B. Then I indicate that meat powder (the US--for unconditioned or "unlearned" stimulus) elicits salivation (the UR--for unconditioned response) because of the manner in which the organism (the dog) is constructed.

C. Then I point out that the CS (bell) comes to elicit the response formerly elicited by the US. But now this response is a CR, because it is elicited by a CS. Once this has been accomplished, I present the definition of classical conditioning: a form of learning in which a previously neutral stimulus (bell) comes to elicit the response (salivation) elicited by another stimulus (meat powder) as a result of being paired repeatedly with the other stimulus.

D. I now mention that all the organism need "do" to be classically conditioned is attend to the pairing of the stimuli.

E. If a student asks whether the US (meat) reinforces the salivation response, I say, "That is an extremely intelligent question, but the concept of reinforcement is applied to operant conditioning, not classical conditioning.

F. Now I explain generalization, discrimination, extinction, and spontaneous recovery in classical conditioning. Emphasize that extinction, in this form of learning, is defined as repeated presentation of the CS (here, the bell) without the US (meat). I usually draw an idealized learning curve on the blackboard, like the following:

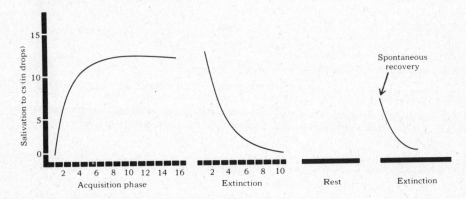

43

III. Operant Conditioning

    A. I begin by asking students to imagine that they are locked in a strange room and they are hungry. Every time they accidentally bump against a spot on one wall, a slice of pizza (burrito, knish, scoop of ice cream--you name it) drops into the room. Soon they learn to tap this spot whenever they feel hungry--because of the effects of the tapping.

    B. Then I describe a rat learning to press a lever in a Skinner box because pressing is reinforced by a food pellet. I emphasize that while a student in a strange room may wonder why tapping led to food, we have no evidence that rats "wonder," and operant conditioning is not described in terms of awareness or consciousness.

    C. Now I define reinforcement, carefully distinguishing it from reward and punishment. As an example of negative reinforcement I point out that anxiety serves as a negative reinforcer when a student studies in order to reduce or eliminate test anxiety. As examples for secondary reinforcement, I point out that students are not born with a desire for money or an A on a test. They must learn that these goals have value.

    D. I point out that extinction, in operant conditioning, is repeated nonreinforced performance of an operant, resulting in discontinuation of that operant.

    E. I mention that in operant conditioning learning occurs when (a) an organism "emits" a response (operant), and (b) the operant is reinforced. Again, there is no mention of thought or consciousness.

IV. A Bridge to Cognitive Learning

    A. As a bridge to cognitive learning, I say that many psychologists believe that it is possible to learn even when an operant is not reinforced (latent learning, E. C. Tolman). Some psychologists think it is also possible to acquire operants even when the learner's do not emit the operants themselves (as in observational learning--watching TV, and so forth.)

DISCUSSION QUESTIONS

1. Students are likely to think of "learning" as an active process through which they attempt to gather and organize information. In order to point out how different this lay notion is from classical and operant conditioning, I like to ask questions such as, "What is the role of thought in classical and operant conditioning?" I emphasize that "thought" plays no role in these paradigms--that classical conditioning results from reinforcement of operants.

2. It is interesting to ask some students to explain to the class what happens during classical and operant conditioning, while other class members are assigned to keeping a list of "mentalistic" terms used by these students. I find that a commonly used mentalistic term in student efforts to explain classical conditioning is "expect" or "expectation." I emphasize that behaviorists explain conditioning through the procedures (pairing, reinforcement) through which learning occurs, not through speculating about what "goes on inside an organism's head."

3. The concept of reinforcement is at first difficult for students to grasp. However, the concept of reinforcement illustrates very well what is meant by an operational definition, if it is explained clearly. I like to ask students to differentiate between rewards and reinforcements. A key difference is that a reward is defined as a pleasant event or stimulus. Pleasure, of course, is subjective; we cannot

know what another person experiences as pleasurable--we can only observe overt behavior. A reinforcer, on the other hand, is defined in terms of its effect on the measurable behavior it follows.

4. I ask students to explain the difference between negative reinforcers and punishments. Again, the mentalistic nature of the punishment concept is highlighted.

5. Examples help students understand principles of conditioning better. I give students examples of classical conditioning and ask them to identify the CS, US, CR, and UR. I provide the operant conditioning examples of (1) saying "Sit" to a dog, (b) pressing the animal's backside down so that it assumes a sitting position, and (c) giving it a piece of food or just patting it on the head while saying "Good boy." After a number of repetitions the dog sits by itself at the command, "Sit." I ask students to identify, in operant conditioning concepts:

   (a) the command "Sit."
   (b) sitting behavior.
   (c) patting the dog on the head and saying "Good boy."

6. Ask students how they would teach the concepts, green, triangle, and standard deviation. Green must be taught by presentation of positive and negative instances (or else by measuring the wave lengths of lights and identifying the band of green.) Triangle may be taught by presentation of positive and negative instances, or else by verbal explanation as a three-sided closed figure. Note that prerequisite concepts for understanding what a triangle is include, "three," "closed," and, through some combination of words or images, a "plane figure." I digress to point out that many classroom learnings are not possible until children have acquired prerequisite concepts. As comedian Bill Cosby noted, you cannot teach a child what two plus two is if the child does not know what "a two" is. Standard deviation must be taught through verbal explanation. What are the concepts with which a person must be familiar in order to understand what is meant by the standard deviation of a distribution?

7. Ask students to explain the meaning of the term extinction in the classical versus operant conditioning paradigms. Focus on the process by which extinction occurs; for example, in classical conditioning the extinction procedure involves repeated presentation of the CS without the US.

8. As a "freedom and dignity" issue, I ask students to imagine that all their personal thoughts are actually conditioned covert responses that are fully determined by a combination of external and internal stimuli. What if their thought, "now I'm choosing exactly what I'm thinking," was just as fully determined. Could this mean that their behavior would be fully determined but that they would have the illusion of being free human beings?

9. I sometimes point to the excerpt from BRAVE NEW WORLD and say to the class, "I guess that looks pretty horrible to us, but couldn't we say our own parents and communities do similar things with us as we're growing up? Don't our parents reward us when we agree with their views and imitate their behavior? Don't they punish us or ignore us if we 'bring home' foreign views expressed by our classmates and teachers?"
   In order to "soften" this notion, I point out that parents are products of their early learning experiences themselves, and that they (usually) want what they believe is best for their children. Also, many parents encourage independent

behavior and free thinking in their children. In BRAVE NEW WORLD, by contrast, the early conditioning was totally cynical, and the effort to shape future likings and behaviors was total and mechanized. Some students will usually now say that their own upbringing was also rather mechanized, especially in terms of certain phrases they were made to repeat in their religious training. At this point I try to remain somewhat neutral and avoid jumping on the students' bandwagon completely. I may make some comment like, "These are the types of issues psychology prompts us to consider."

10. I ask students to imagine how their lives would be different if drugs or other methods were developed that permitted us to retain information after attending to it just once, rather than having to repeat it many times.

MATERIALS FOR STUDENT DISTRIBUTION

Handout 4.1: Effects of Positive and Negative Reinforcers

This handout will help students learn to differentiate between positive and negative reinforcers. It helps them also differentiate between punishments and negative reinforcers by showing that negative reinforcers, like positive reinforcers, also strengthen responses. Of course, it may be that the students would characterize the examples of negative reinforcers as punishing; however, reinforcers are defined in terms of their demonstrated effects upon behavior, not in terms of inferred subjective experiences.

Handout 4.2:   Behavior Patterns Resulting from Four Intermittent Reinforcement Schedules

This handout enables the instructor to discuss some of the characteristics of the four basic types of schedules of (intermittent) reinforcement in greater depth. While it is understood that a true behavioral explanation of the effects of these schedules avoids any suggestion of mentalism, mentalistic examples followed by a quick disclaimer seem reasonably effective as pedagogical procedures.

The example of studying for exams is given to illustrate the fixed-interval schedules. The fixed-interval schedule is characterized by "cramming," in which the student studies little following an exam, but builds studying behavior just prior to the occurrence of the next, perfectly predictable exam. It should be emphasized that this response pattern also holds for rats that are reinforced for bar-pressing after a specified interval has passed.

The example of looking into one's mailbox for a dividend check is used to illustrate the variable-interval schedule. When checks are mailed only part of the time, the response of looking for them in one's mailbox is reinforced on a variable-interval schedule. This uncertainty (mentalistic term!) leads to daily (or several times daily) checking in the mailbox.

Payment for piece work illustrates the fixed-ratio schedule when workers are paid after producing a certain number of items, 10, 20, or 100, there is a generally high rate of response. However, there tends to be a brief pause after a reinforcement, perhaps because the first few responses following a reinforcement are not associated with reinforcement so strongly as later responses. Given the generally high rate of responding, it is apparent that this sort of payment system is reasonably attractive to employers as a measure of increasing productivity. Many companies are also now using bonus systems for pieces of work completed above a certain minimum, which also leads to higher productivity.

In variable–ratio schedules, the occurrence of reinforcement also depends on the number of responses performed, but the incidence varies from a particular average value. If the ratio is 25 to 1, reinforcements may occur, for example, after 10, 30, 35, 15, 40, 5 and 40 responses. Such schedules, as with slot–machine payments, often lead to high, constant response levels, apparently because it has been learned that reinforcement may follow any response. Observation of many slot–machine gamblers in Atlantic City and Las Vegas will quickly convince anyone that many of these individuals continue to pump their change into the machine quite mechanically, hardly pausing even when they "win big."

Handout 4.3: Principles for Using Punishment

The text indicates that many learning theorists suggest that punishment has certain inadequacies as a method for decreasing the frequency of undesired behaviors. However, as shown in this handout, if one is going to use punishment, there are seven principles that make punishment more effective: (1) avoiding inadequate punishment, (2) finding a punishment that suits the offense, (3) requiring an incompatible escape response, (4) punishing immediately, (5) reinstating the circumstances when punishment cannot be delivered immediately, (6) avoiding rewards after punishment, (7) providing an acceptable alternative to the punished behavior.

In using this handout, indicate that under each principle for using punishment there are three examples and then a problem. What do students suggest as methods for solving these problems that are consistent with the principles for using punishment? Below are some possible answers to these problems:

1. Verbal reprimand but no change in grade may encourage continued cheating.
2. Student caught turning in someone else's term paper should work for the committee that reviews grievances against students.
3. Could the instructor convince students who consistently get low grades to stop watching TV until their grades improve?
4. Could proctors outside doors direct students who come to class late to one rear entrance and back seats only?
5. Students caught plagiarizing should bring in plagiarized material and show instructor exactly where it came from.
6. No provision of a second chance, a second exam, or an extra assignment, for students who flunk tests.
7. An instructor can find out from such a student the areas of living in which he or she excels and encourage satisfaction of n Ach there.

Handout 4.4: A Drug to Make People Smarter?

Newsweek (May 4, 1971) report on research with the hormone vasopressin as a "memory enhancer."

Handout 4.5: A "Simple" Memory Test

Which penny is accurate? Most people fail this "simple" test.

CHAPTER 5

MOTIVATION AND EMOTION

LEARNING OBJECTIVES

After reading this chapter the student should be able to

1. Define and differentiate among the concepts of motive, need, incentive, and drive.
2. List and define the needs in Maslow's hierarchy.
3. Distinguish between primary and secondary drives.
4. Explain the concept of homeostasis and show how it relates to various motives.
5. Summarize research concerning the role of the hypothalamus in hunger drive.
6. Summarize research concerning the physiological and psychological determinants of obesity.
7. Summarize research concerning differences between internal and external eaters.
8. Explain how hormones regulate the thirst drive.
9. Explain why salty pretzels make people (and goats) thirsty.
10. Explain the effects of hormones and electrical stimulation to the brain on sexual behavior in lower animals.
11. Summarize research concerning the effects of pornography.
12. Define homosexuality.
13. Discuss cultural attitudes that foster a climate that "supports" rape.
14. Discuss sexual changes that occur with aging.
15. Summarize research evidence showing that (a) maternal behavior is controlled mechanically in lower animals, and (b) maternal behavior is (probably) not a primary drive in humans.
16. Summarize the effects of sensory deprivation.
17. Define sensation-seeking and relate the concept to the concept of physiological arousal.
18. Define optimal arousal and explain the Yerkes-Dodson Law.
19. Define each of the social motives listed in the text, and summarize research on the needs for achievement, affiliation, and power.
20. Define emotion and explain how emotions can serve as responses, motives, and goals.
21. List some physiological, situational, and cognitive components of emotions of fear, anger, and depression.
22. Explain the theoretical rationale behind the use of the polygraph as a lie detector.
23. List commonalities and differences in the expression of emotions in various cultures.
24. Explain the facial feedback hypothesis of emotion.
25. Explain and evaluate the James-Lange, Cannon-Bard, and Schachter-Singer theories of emotion.

LECTURE NOTES

Lecture: Aggression: A Major Issue in Human Motivation

I. Introduction

   A. I usually introduce this topic in motivation by asking questions such as the following: Why are there wars? Are people innately aggressive? Will aggression always be with us? I insist that students attempt to support their feelings with scientific evidence.
   B. Then I attempt to arrive at a definition of aggression with the class. Issues that usually arise are: Can one be aggressive in behavior if one does not intend to harm another? Can aggression be verbal as well as physical? Can we label competitive, hard-driving business behavior as "aggressive?" I point out that many psychologists today label hard-driving behavior "Type A," and that some psychologists consider outspoken, self-advancing behavior as "assertive," not aggressive.

II. Approaches to Understanding Aggressive Behavior

   A. Comparative research suggests that many species (fish, birds, rodents, and others) will behave aggressively when exposed to a "releasing" stimulus (such as a robin's red breast) or to a painful stimulus (for example, electric shock). In lower animals, electrical stimulation of parts of the brain may result in a stereotyped aggressive response, although this is not true with monkeys, and presumably not true with humans.
   B. From the psychoanalytic perspective, aggressive impulses are inevitable, often representing displacement of aggressive impulses toward loved ones. Neurotic anxiety may represent efforts to keep such impulses repressed. Freud (and Lorenz) suggested catharsis of such impulses. But research in catharsis suggests that "catharsis" of aggressive impulses may be effective only when persons believe their aggression is justified--showing that a mechanical, value-free venting of aggressive impulses probably does not occur.
   C. According to social learning theory, aggressive operants are acquired through operant conditioning and/or observational learning. In operant conditioning emission of an aggressive operant (whether emission results from trial-and-error, physical guidance, or whatever) is reinforced. In observational learning aggressive operants are acquired though they are not emitted and reinforced.
      (1) Some rewards for aggressive operants: removal of threat from aggressor; parental or peer approval; reduction of arousal in instances in which aggression seems justified:
      (2) Some ways in which TV violence may contribute to aggression: (a) increasing viewer's level of arousal; (b) acting as a catalyst; (c) teaching aggressive skills; (d) desensitizing viewer to violence.
      (3) Question: Should aggressive behavior be punished in children? (Possible direction for answers: Why would Skinner suggest that instead of punishment we encourage alternate responses to provocation and reinforce them?)
      (4) Social learning theory summary: Probability of an aggressive response increases as a result of (a) heightened arousal (as through provocation); (b) aggressive behavioral competencies; (c) positive expected outcome; and (d) consistency of aggressive behavior with one's values.
   D. Aggression and Crowd Behavior: It may be useful to foreshadow Chapter 11 by stating that a social psychological approach emphasizes social deter-

minants of behavior. In a crowd, factors increasing the probability of mob behavior are (a) deindividuation; and (b) diffusion of responsibility.

DISCUSSION QUESTiONS

1. It is interesting to have students track their eating behavior for a few days--to write down the time of day, their location, whom they were with, what they were doing at the time, what their mood was like, their impression of why they ate, and their reaction to eating. Students may also be encouraged to use calorie counters to estimate the number of calories they take in per day. Then, in class, have them discuss what they discovered about their eating patterns. Some students will find that they ate because a friend said, "Let's get something to eat," because they were bored, or because it was the time of day to eat a meal. All of these, of course, are "external" triggers of eating behavior.

2. Before assigning the chapter, it is interesting to promote a class discussion around the question, "Do women make natural mothers?" If students are unclear about the import of the question, it can be phrased, "Well, is there such a thing as a maternal instinct in human beings?" Each time a student presents (usually ancecdotal) "evidence" for a maternal instinct. I ask the class if there is another possible interpretation of the anecdote. The class will usually rather readily come to see that it is possible that a socialization process accounts for maternal behavior in humans.

3. Following discussion of question #2. I often ask the class, "What type of experiment would have to be done to determine whether a certain type of behavior is instinctive in human beings?" Gradually the class arrives at the recognition that this type of experiment would be unethical with humans. Thus, they can understand why we make efforts to generalize to human beings from organisms most similar to humans--that is, higher animals, especially monkeys and apes.

4. In order to introduce emotion, I will ask students, "How do you know when you are afraid? How do you know when you are in love?" Students usually focus on the signs of bodily arousal (rapid heart beat and so on) that accompany these emotions, although there is some tendency to report fantasizing about a loved person, or the desire to be with or care for a loved person.
   If we begin with the question about fear, and then move on to love, I often ask students to differentiate between the two emotions. They may be hard-pressed to do so on the basis of physical sensations, unless they include the area of sexual arousal. This problem leads quite naturally into a discussion of the situational determinants of emotions.

5. Sometimes, as I'm sure you've discovered, discussing an issue which does not seem directly related to a controversial subject elicits more open and informal dialogue. On issues of rape, gender differences and homosexuality, students often take "positions" rather than analyzing the subject. These positions sometimes mask the underlying attitudes with which they (and we) have been socialized. I have found that raising the question: why not have unisex bathroom facilities in schools? provokes a discussion which, so far, inevitably brings out the students' assumptions about the human body, gender identity and sexuality.

6. It may be useful to remind the students as they discuss pornography, its effects and/or assumed effects that there is a long cross-cultural history to sexually stimulating material. This piece of information disallows reliance on such argu-

ments as "We're a completely decadent society! That's why there's pornography." It can also help emphasize the importance of context in the definition of a piece of material. Is the painting of the rape of the Sabines pornographic? If the characters in the painting were updated, would it be pornographic? Is the <u>Kama Sutra</u> different from the <u>Joy of Sex</u>?

7. I like to ask the class why they believe certain people are homosexual. Early in the discussion it becomes clear that some class members view homosexuality as a matter of personal choice and tend to link it to some sort of vague concept of rebelliousness. At this point I like to ask the class whether they recall choosing their heterosexuality (assuming that the majority of the class is heterosexual.)

Homosexual organizations have recently been formed on many campuses, and these organizations are usually more than pleased to send representatives to classes so that students may ask them questions. I have been surprised, I admit, at how hostile some questions can be--for example, "When did you first stop caring how much you hurt your parents?" When I moderate these discussions, I find that some representatives of campus homosexual groups can handle such questions very well, but that at other times I have to point out that certain questions are biased and cannot be answered directly.

MATERIALS FOR STUDENT DISTRIBUTION

Handout 5.1: 118 Pound Woman Lifts 4,500 Pound Car

This Associated Press item (December 6, 1979) appears supportive of the Yerkes-Doson Law, which specifies that persons carry out simple tasks such as lifting a car, most efficiently when they are experiencing high levels of motivation, such as the woman's emotional response to observing the trapped child.

News items presented in these handouts may be abbreviated versions of the originals, but they have not been otherwise altered. Thus it is advised that instructors read them carefully to determine whether certain statements are scientifically unsound and should thus receive commentary in the classroom.

Handout 5.2: The Pleasant Events Schedule

The text indicates that Peter Lewinsohn and his colleagues at the University of Oregon have done pioneering work in the use of pleasant events to combat feelings of depression. Lewinsohn's view is that pleasant events are incompatible with feelings of depression, and his research has suggested that in many cases feelings of depression can be alleviated by purposefully engaging in a number of pleasant events each day.

Of course we vary in what we find pleasant, boring, and unpleasant. Lewinsohn has found that we can each construct a personal list of pleasant events from two 160-item checklists constructed at the University of Oregon. Handout 5.2 is an adaptation of these two 160-item checklists, reducing them to 114 items. Students can use the abbreviated list (from Rathus, S. A. and Nevid, J.S. ADJUSTMENT AND GROWTH: THE CHALLENGES OF LIFE. New York: Holt, Rinehart and Winston, 1986) either to enrich the quality of their daily lives or to cope with feelings of depression. They may check items that they find pleasant or have found pleasant in the past, and then simply arrange to schedule some of them into their daily lives. Some require more effort and preparation than others, but it may be reasonable to try to schedule three to five of them into each day's activities.

Handout 5.3:   Counting Calories

Whether people use diet pills or exercise, scientific evidence consistently shows that the way to lose weight is burn up more calories than we consume.   Dieters must thus become aware of how many calories they tend to consume in a day and how many calories they burn.   Students who wish to count the calories they consume may purchase any one of a number of good, inexpensive calorie counters.   Then they simply track the calories they consume on a daily basis.

Handout 5.3 will help them determine how many calories they burn up each day. The first chart indicates approximately how many calories they will burn according to the activity they engage in and their present body weight.   Heavier people burn more calories as they engage in the same activity as a lighter person--it is like driving a heavier car the same distance at the same speed.   The second chart shows how many calories are burned in a typical day by "Paul," a fictitious office worker.   If Paul burns up more calories than he eats, he will lose weight.   If he eats more than he burns, he will gain weight.   How much?   He can find out by using the formula, 3,500 calories = one pound of body weight.   Thus, if he burns 250 calories more a day than he takes in, he will lose one pound in fourteen days (two weeks).

These charts are taken from ADJUSTMENT AND GROWTH: THE CHALLENGES OF LIFE (Rathus, S. A. and Nevid, J.S. New York: Holt, Rinehart & Winston, 1986).

CHAPTER 6

DEVELOPMENTAL PSYCHOLOGY

LEARNING OBJECTIVES

After reading this chapter the student should be able to

1. Describe the process of conception.
2. Define the important developmental concepts of nature, nurture, stage, and matura-tion.
3. Reproduce the outline of the major stage theories of development (Table 6.I in the text).
4. Differentiate the period of the ovum from the embryonic and fetal periods.
5. Describe the effects of various chemical and other agents on unborn children (Table 6.2 in text).
6. Describe the major events of the three trimesters of prenatal development, and explain the role of sex hormones on prenatal sexual differentiation.
7. List and describe the major reflexes present at birth.
8. Describe the development of vision, hearing, smell, taste, and pain in infants.
9. Summarize Harlow's research with infant monkeys, explaining its implications for attachment and the effects of social deprivation in humans.
10. Explain the ethological view of attachment.
11. Summarize the effects of day care.
I2. Summarize the research of Kagan and Skeels & Dye concerning the effects and reversibility of social deprivation.
I3. Explain biological, psychoanalytic, social learning and cognitive approaches to understanding identification and sex typing.

14. List Piaget's four stages of cognitive development, and describe the major characteristics of each.
15. Define Piaget's concepts of schema, assimilation, accommodation, object permanency, egocentrism, and conservation.
16. List and explain Kohlberg's levels and stages of moral development.
17. Define and differentiate between the concepts of puberty and adolescence.
18. Summarize the physical changes that take place during adolescence.
19. Explain Erikson's concept of ego identity.
20. Describe the major crises and challenges of young adulthood, middle adulthood, and late adulthood.
21. Describe theories of aging and the physical and psychological changes that occur during late adulthood.
22. List and explain Kubler-Ross's five stages of dying.

LECTURE NOTES

Lecture: Piaget's Approach to Cognitive Development

I. Introduction: Basic Principles of Piaget's Approach

    A. Development occurs in stages; it is not continuous.
    B. People think differently in different stages. Children are not just little, less-knowledgeable adults.
    C. The sequence of stages is invariable for all children in all cultures, although different children may develop at different rates and not everyone reaches the formal operational stage.
    D. There is an emphasis on the process of maturation. Children's development of conservation, for example, cannot be hastened by instruction. This, I emphasize, is Piaget's most controversial assumption.

II. Basic Terms In Piaget's Approach

    A. Schema, schemata (or schemas)
    B. Assimilation
    C. Accomodation
    D. "True intelligence"--the harmonious interaction of assimilation and accomodation.

III. Definitions and Landmarks of Piaget's Stages of Development

    A. Sensorimotor stage--about zero to two years.
       (1) Lack of language, symbols, or mental representation at first.
       (2) Intentional behavior begins (might compare child's making interesting events last or repeat with operant conditioning; but Piaget, of course, attributes purpose to the child, whereas behaviorists attempt to avoid mentalistic concepts).
       (3) Object permanence acquired at about nine months.
       (4) Rudiments of language gradually acquired.
    B. Preoperational stage--about two to seven years.
       (1) Egocentric mental representation. Child shows animism and artificialism. (Students appreciate several examples.)
       (2) Lack of conservation. (Describe experiments.)
       (3) Moral judgments are objective--focusing on the amount of damage done rather than on the intentions (motives) of a wrongdoer.

C. Concrete operational stage—seven to twelve years.
   (1) Conservation and reversibility concepts are present: child centers on two aspects of situation simultaneously.
   (2) Thought becomes less egocentric.
   (3) Child understands relational concepts—longer versus shorter, lightest to heaviest in a series.
   (4) Moral judgments become subjective, focusing on motives of a wrong-doer.
D. Formal operational stage—twelve years and older.
   (1) Deductive reasoning emerges: person can understand syllogistic thinking (deducing from premises).
   (2) Thought is abstract: specific plans and judgments are derived from principles, as in geometry and philosophy.
   (3) New egocentrism can emerge as adolescent, who can now derive "right" and "wrong" from moral principles, may become impatient with adult focus on "shades of gray."

DISCUSSION QUESTIONS

1. What are the implications of being able to greatly increase the chances of determining the sex of one's child? What if we could completely determine the sex of our children? Is it possible that parental choice of boys and girls would tend to even out in the long run, or might there be too many children of one sex and not enough of the other? Are there implications for the maintenance of the institution of marriage? For the incidence of homosexuality? At some point might the government legislate against using sex-determination procedures? If pinpointing the time of ovulation and deciding when to have intercourse can practically guarantee the sex of the child, what types of measures would a restrictive government have to take in order to safeguard against sex selection? Students can give some rather far-out science-fiction types of answers to this question—such as methods that prevent people from reproducing except under the direction of the government-controlled reproduction centers.

2. Consider the recent development of "test-tube babies." Can students describe the procedures that might be used to undertake conception outside of the mother's body? The point here is to have them consider where the egg cell would be taken from. Then what type of environment might the egg cell and fertilized ovum require? About how much time does the zygote have before it would have to be returned to the mother? To what location(s) might it be returned? Answers to these questions require knowledge of the role of the fallopian tubes and the period of the ovum.

3. Can students recall "early socialization messages" they received that encouraged them to undertake certain sex roles? Can boys recall being urged to be "a man's man?" Not to back away from fights? To be aggressive and competitive? Can girls recall being told how important it was to "marry right" as the great achievement in life? That they must be attractive and act like "little ladies?" These discussions sometimes evoke a great deal of emotion from the students, particularly if they have chafed under these early gender socialization messages.

4. Ask students if draft evaders during the Vietnam War were simply afraid or were behaving according to a high level of moral judgment (according to Kohlberg). Many of these men were faced with a dilemma in which their personal values and sense of justice conflicted with a law. In discussing this issue, I try

to point out that all these men were individuals and that some of them may have derived their conduct through a difficult personal crisis involving such a conflict of values, while others may have seized the opportunity engendered by public controversy simply to avoid serving. Thus similar behavior may have quite different motives, and many of these evaders may have been acting quite less morally than others. (I have found, to my amazement, that many young students today are barely familiar with this issue!) For an article which relates some of the moral dilemmas of Vietnam with their psychic aftermath ten years later, see "The War That Has No Ending", DISCOVER, June, 1985, p. 44ff.

5. Adolescence has been characterized as a period of "storm and stress." What types of adolescent experiences have class members had? Has adolescence been stressful? How so? I usually tell my classes that the ensuing discussion will be rated PG, not R or X.

6. What is the role of raising children in marriage? Is child-rearing the major reason for a marriage? What are some reasons that many young people today have decided to delay having children, perhaps to have only one child, or not to have children at all? What does the class think of people who decide not to have children? Are they selfish, unbalanced, "weird?" Are there "unhealthy" reasons for deciding to have children?

7. Since American society is particularly age conscious, it may be helpful to take note of a few points of cultural and historical relativity to facilitate analysis. For instance, you may wish to point out that every society defines appropriate behavior for different age grades, but not every society treats age chronologically. Girls and women may have different roles, but you may not become a woman until you marry, whether you marry at 13 or 30.

8. Attributes associated with age differ for men and women. You might want to ask your students to do a comparative analysis of age references in the newspaper or magazines. They may find that male executives in their early 40s are usually considered to be young, an attitude reflected in the adjectives used to describe them. Females are usually still predominantly mentioned in fashion and home or social sections where adjectives reflecting youth are used to characterize women in their 20s. What kind of impact might these cultural expectations have on men and women.

9. What do students see for themselves when they become middle-aged. Most students have very little idea as to what they may be doing or feeling when they are in their forties or fifties. Moreover, human longevity has changed through history, while not all age-related role expectations have changed in response. In Massachusetts in 1850 the average life expectancy was 38.3 for men and 40.5 for women; it is now approximately 70 for men and 78 for women. For an interesting discussion you may wish to ask how our current concepts and expectations for middle age and old age would fit into our country's past? How do they think these same concepts will change (or remain the same) in the future?

MATERIALS FOR STUDENT DISTRIBUTION

Handout 6.1:   Three Moral Dilemmas

This handout includes three moral dilemmas taken from ADJUSTMENT AND GROWTH: THE CHALLENGES OF LIFE (Rathus, S.A., and Nevid, J. S. New York: Holt, Rinehart and Winston, 1986). They can be used to illustrate Lawrence Kohlberg's levels of moral development. In each case human needs are placed in opposition to social rules or legal codes. What do students believe to be the "right" course of action in each case? Why?

Students may vaguely recollect the Chad Green case. Chad died of Leukemia in Tijuana. Whether court-ordered treatment in the United States could have saved his life is obviously a matter of speculation that cannot be scientifically demonstrated. His parents, of course, report that they believe they acted morally because their motive was to save their son from what they believed was harmful treatment, even though it involved kidnapping him and he died after several months in Mexico.

News items presented in these handouts may be abbreviated versions of the originals, but they have not been otherwise altered. Thus it is advised that instructors read them carefully to determine whether certain statements are scientifically unsound and should thus receive commentary in the classroom.

Handout 6.2:   Attitudes toward Aging Test

This test will help the class discover whether they hold stereotypical images of the aging. Students can score their own tests. The key for scoring is very simple: all test items are false.

Handout 6.3:   Facts on Aging

Some research findings on aging which may prove useful for discussion.

Handout 6.4:   Kids and Trauma

A NEWSWEEK (January 18, 1982) report on research by Jerome Kagan and others that suggests that early traumatic events may not leave "psychic scars" as deep as had been feared.

Handout 6.5:   In Vitro Research

In Vitro fertilization has stimulated a great deal of research and raised many controversial issues. This handout touches on a few of them: For example, if private industry does embryo research, will it "own" the results of any fertilization? Might there be a different feeling of "self" for the person knowing he or she was conceived outside a human womb? If we can repair defective genes, which genes shall be declared defective and who shall decide which embryos are repaired?

CHAPTER 7

PERSONALITY

LEARNING OBJECTIVES

After reading this chapter the student should be able to

1. Define personality.
2. Explain why Freud's psychoanalytic theory is described as psychodynamic.
3. Summarize research evidence for and against the view that catharsis of aggressive impulses decreases the probability of subsequent aggressive behavior.
4. Describe the development of Freud's psychic structures and explain which one(s) is/are conscious.
5. List Freud's five stages of psychosexual development and describe the major events of each.
6. List and explain the origins of so-called oral and anal personality traits.
7. Explain the implications of the Oedipus and Electra complexes for adult sexual behavior and the assuming of sex roles.
8. Discuss the penis envy controversy, and why Freud's views are criticized by many women.
9. Critically evaluate Freud's psychoanalytic theory.
10. Explain differences between the psychoanalytic views of Jung and Freud.
11. Explain differences between the psychoanalytic views of Adler and Freud.
12. Explain differences between the psychoanalytic views of Erikson and Freud.
13. List and define Erikson's stages of psychosocial development.
14. Define and contrast the concepts of traits and types.
15. Explain the contributions of Allport, Cattell, Hippocrates and Sheldon to trait theory.
16. Explain the differences between radical behaviorism and social learning theory.
17. List and explain the roles of personal and situational variables in social learning theory.
18. Explain the contributions of Carl Rogers to self theory.
19. Define and explain the relationships between the terms self, self-actualization, self-concept, and self-esteem.
20. Critically evaluate trait theory (including type theory), social learning theory and self theory.
21. Define what is meant by sex roles and sex-role stereotypes.
22. Describe the stereotypical masculine and feminine sex-role stereotypes in our culture.
23. Summarize research concerning the effects of sexism on women who show talent and who join the professional ranks. Summarize the findings of the Broverman study on sex-role stereotypes and judgments of mental health.
24. Define "fear of success" and summarize research concerning women (and men) and fear of success.
25. Define psychological androgny, and summarize research concerning psychologically androgynous individuals.
26. Summarize research concerning cognitive and personality sex differences.

LECTURE NOTES

Lecture: Psychoanalytic Theory

I. Basic Assumptions of Psychoanalytic Theory

   A. Behavior is determined (doctrine of psychic determinism).
   B. People are largely unaware of the real motives for their behavior.
   C. The core tendency is that people attempt to gratify basic instincts in ways
       that permit them to avoid social and, eventually, self-condemnation.

II. The Geography of the Mind

   A. I often introduce these concepts by relating Freud's experiences with pa-
       tients with hysterical conversion disorders (like glove anesthesia), which
       convinced him of unconscious processes.
   B. Definition of and distinction between conscious, preconscious, and uncon-
       scious parts of the mind.

III. The Structure of Personality

   A. The id: a mental or psychic structure present at birth; "cauldron of seething
       excitations"; source of motivation; operates according to pleasure principle.
   B. The ego: develops through experience; coping behavior plus conscious sense
       of self; reality principle; ego defense mechanisms protect ego from anxiety:
       (1) Denial: not recognizing a threat.
       (2) Repression: ejecting unacceptable thoughts and impulses from conscious-
            ness.
       (3) Projection: attributing one's own unacceptable impulses to others.
       (4) Rationalization: justification of unacceptable behavior.
       (5) Reaction formation: expression of emotion opposite to that really
            experienced (experienced in the id).
       (6) Intellectualization: perceiving threats emotionlessly in order to reduce
            their impact.
       (7) Sublimation: redirection of unacceptable instincts into acceptable
            social or cultural activity.
   C. The superego: develops in middle childhood through identification. "Con-
       science." Can flood ego with feelings of guilt and shame: "moral anxiety."
   D. I now introduce "intrapsychic conflict," picturing the ego as attempting
       to walk on a tightrope--balanced precariously in an effort to meet id de-
       mands but avoid moral anxiety.

IV. Psychosexual Development

   A. Basic introductory concepts: eros, libido (psychosexual energy), psycho-
       sexual development, erogeneous zones, stage theory of development, fixa-
       tion.
   B. Five stages of psychosexual development:
       (1) Oral stage: first year of life; importance of weaning; concept of oral
            gratification; (optional: oral passive versus oral aggressive;) oral traits,
            like dependency, depression, gullibility, optimism versus pessimism.
       (2) Anal stage: second to third year of life; importance of toilet training;
            development of anal traits that are retentive or expulsive. A reference

58

to Tony Randall and Jack Klugman in the TV series <u>The Odd Couple</u> is usually helpful.

   (3) Phallic stage: about three to five or six; careful delineation of the Oedipus complex and the Electra complex. I often retell the story of the Greek king Oedipus here. To develop the concepts further, I present the Freudian explanations of male and female homosexuality, if there is time--emphasizing the weakness of actual evidence for these views. I find it important to go through the Freudian view of the assertive, competitive businesswoman, and to present counterveiling views, especially those of Karen Horney. Students find Freud's beliefs concerning two types of female orgasm fascinating, especially when they then learn of evidence suggesting only one type of orgasm from the laboratories of Masters and Johnson.

   (4) Latency stage: about six through puberty. I usually begin with a joke to the effect that after five or six years of strenuous sexual activity and endless yearnings, kids now finally have a chance to rest for a while. But then evidence is presented that children at these ages are sexually active, playing "doctor" and experimenting.

   (5) Genital stage: puberty and beyond, reemergence of Oedipal urges and displacement of incestuous impulses onto appropriate members of the opposite sex. I emphasize the traditionalist bias to Freud's thinking that the life instincts are somehow meant to culminate in reproduction (within an intimate relationship that provides a nurturant setting for child-rearing).

V. Evaluation

   A. Other psychoanalysts have suggested that motives can stem from the ego as well as the id.

   B. Other psychoanalysts believe that Freud overemphasized the importance of sexual instincts.

   C. Freud uses many concepts (for example, psychic structures, repression) that cannot be measured directly.

   D. Freud's explanations for behavior were generally post hoc; psychoanalytic theory does not predict behavior very well.

DISCUSSION QUESTIONS

1. Ask women in the class if they were ever treated as being unusual or strange if they expressed the view that they wanted to assert themselves in the business world. If the class has developed a feeling of closeness, it may be possible to ask women if they ever felt jealous of their brothers or of other boys. I would suggest making it clear that you are not speaking of penis-envy, but perhaps an envy of the types of expectations parents seemed to have for male as opposed to female children. I then ask the men in the class whether they have sometimes felt that women had it easier because less seems to be expected of them (in the achieving sense). This can often lead to a balanced discussion of ways in which each sex envies the other for an attribute legitimated for one sex only.

2. What are the implications of Freud's theory of personality for great artists, writers, architects, doctors and so forth? I lead the class to recognize that from the traditional Freudian perspective, these accomplishments are viewed as defenses against anxiety, or ways of channeling unacceptable impulses into socially acceptable modes of conduct. In other words, Freudian theory tends to take the nobility

out of acting nobly. This interpretation is logical if one believes that all motivation stems from the id. I point out that many Neofreudians believe that motivation can also stem from the (conscious) ego--thus allowing for the presence of fully conscious, pro-social motives.

3. What does Erikson mean by the stage of generativity versus stagnation? Does this mean that it is psychologically healthy during the middle years to raise children, and unhealthy to decide not to raise children? I usually note that Erikson was indeed rather traditional in his personal beliefs, and valued highly the family as an institution within which to raise children. However, Erikson did allow for other types of generativity--teaching, writing, and so on.

4. In order to determine whether the class understands what are meant by person and situational variables in social learning theory, I like to offer an example, such as the following, and ask the class to indicate what person and situational variables will determine whether Johnny behaves aggressively:
    "Johnny walks into a bar with his girlfriend. A man walks up to his girlfriend and says, 'You're a good looker. What are you doing with a creep like this?'"
    One person variable involves behavioral competencies or skills, and Johnny is more likely to respond aggressively if he possesses these competencies and so forth.

5. I ask the class how it would be possible to demonstrate that people do (or do not) have a primary drive for self-actualization. For instance, is such a drive universal? If so, it might be suggestive, though not conclusive evidence, of such a drive; however, many people do seem to drift along rather than pursue some objective actively. Rogers might suggest that people drift as a reaction to receiving conditional positive regard at an early age. But it is a fallacy to interpret negative instances (for instance, examples of such drifting) as proof of a positive point. I usually conclude that Rogers' view remains to be demonstrated. I mention that a few learning theorists regard self-actualization as a secondary drive that is acquired by same, but that is far from universal.

MATERIALS FOR STUDENT DISTRIBUTION

Handout 7.l: The Family Circus

While this cartoon has no scientific value and need not apply to the Oedipus complex, it is sure to earn a few laughs from your classes when you discuss the Oedipus complex.

Handout 7.2: Measuring Self-Actualization

These nine items are taken from E. L. Shostrum's PERSONAL ORIENTATION INVENTORY (San Diego: Educational and Industrial Testing Service, l963), which is constructed to assess Carl Rogers' and Abraham Maslow's construct of self-actualization. Answers in the direction of self-actualization are: l b, 2 b, 3 a, 4 b, 5 b, 6 a, 7a, 8 a, 9 b.
    While these nine items will not permit class members a very reliable measure of thier own self-actualization, they can serve as a device to encourage discussion of the characteristics of the self-actualizer. You can ask, "What aspect of self-actualization is measured by each item?" Here are some possible answers:

Item I.   Living for the present moment.
Item 2:   Autonomy.
Item 3:   Spontaneity.
Item 4:   Independence and ability to tolerate differentness in others.
Item 5:   Genuineness.
Item 6:   Acceptance of feelings of sexual arousal (not to be equated with con-
           sistently acting them out).
Item 7:   Acceptance of ambiguousness.
Item 8:   Acceptance of negative feelings.
Item 9:   Ability to express feelings.

Handout 7.3:   The ANDRO Scale--A Measure of Psychological Androgyny

This scale assesses the degree to which students adhere to traditional sex roles--
whether they are, in the words of Stanford psychologist Sandra Bem, "chesty males"
and "fluffy females." Some do, of course, and a few are "cross-typed"--that is, masculine women and feminine men, at least according to descriptors of the stereotypes.
But Sandra Bem has found about 35 percent of college students to be psychologically
androgynous, or capable of displaying behaviors deemed representative of both traditional masculine and feminine sex roles, depending on the requirements of the situation.
It is Bem's view that such individuals are generally more adaptive.
This particular ANDRO scale was developed by Berzins, Welling, and Wetter (1977).

Handout 7.4:   Scoring Key for the ANDRO Scale

This key permits students to score their response to the ANDRO scale as masculine
or feminine. They may then rank themselves among a college sample for both traits,
and may compare their scores to those of various groups of respondents shown in the
figure that follows the scoring key.

CHAPTER 8

ABNORMAL BEHAVIOR

LEARNING OBJECTIVES

After reading this chapter the student should be able to

I. Discuss the distinction between insanity and abnormal behavior.
2. Discuss why the insanity pleas is so controversial.
3. Define abnormal behavior using the six criteria (standards) listed in the textbook.
4. List, describe, and compare several models for understanding abnormal behavior
    (including two versions of the medical model).
5. Discuss several differences between the DSM-II and the DSM-III, including the
    treatment of the concept of neurosis and the issues of diagnostic reliability.
6. List three major types of anxiety disorders and describe the symptoms of each.
7. Contrast the psychoanalytic, behavioral, social learning, and cognitive views of
    phobias.
8. List three major types of dissociative disorders and describe the symptoms of
    each.

9. List two major types of somatoform disorders (conversion disorder and hypochondriasis) and describe the symptoms of each.
10. Explain why conversion disorder was once labeled an "hysterical" disorder.
11. Explain differences between normal depression, dysthymic disorder (or depressive neurosis), major depressive episode, and bipolar affective disorder.
12. Discuss various theoretical approaches to understanding the causes of depression. Discuss evidence concerning the roles of learned helplessness, attributional style, and possible biochemical factors.
13. Differentiate between schizophrenia and schizophreniform disorders.
14. Describe the symptoms of schizophrenia, including those of subtypes of schizophrenia.
15. Discuss various theoretical approaches to the causes of schizophrenia. Discuss evidence concerning possible genetic and biochemical factors in schizophrenia.
16. List several characteristics of the sociopath.
17. Summarize research on the origins of sociopathy, emphasizing the role of anxiety (or lack of anxiety, to be more accurate?).
18. Define each of the pscyhosexual disorders presented in the text.
19. Present various psychological explanations of the "Paraphilias."
20. Define drug abuse, alcoholism, two types of dependence, addiction, tolerance, and abstinence syndrome.
21. Sumarize research concerning the possible causes of drug dependence.
22. Describe the effects of alcohol, including the abstinence syndrome for alcohol, and delirium tremens (DTs).
23. Describe the effects of marijuana, amphetamines, opiates, cocaine, barbituates and methaqualone, LSD and other hallucinogenics.
24. Indicate which of the drugs in item 15 are addictive, and discuss problems in dealing with their abstinence syndromes.

LECTURE NOTES

Lecture: Introduction to Abnormal Behavior

I.   Examples of Abnormal Behavior

   A.   Recount the story of William Milligan, asking the questions: Was his behavior abnormal? What do we mean by abnormal? (Is it sufficient to be different? Einstein was different.) How do we account for it? What do we do about it?
   B.   It is possible to use a handout from this Instructor's Manual with another instance of abnormal behavior.
   C.   When this course is being taught, there may be a recent news item that can be brought in. Students may also remember the Jim Jones suicides in Guyana (People's Temple).

II.   Historical View of Abnormal Behavior

   A.   Demonism has been the central historical view from the Stone Age through the Middle Ages. Even now, don't people often explain unusual behavior by saying, "Something just got into me."? What of "Geraldine's" expression, "The devil made me do it."?
   B.   Students are usually fascinated by the concepts of possession, exorcism, witchcraft, and so on. There seems, in fact, to have been an upsurge in

public willingness to entertain these ideas as evidenced by many box office hits, e.g., the Exorcist, The Amityville Horror, all the Stephen King films, Friday the 13th, Children of the Corn, etc. How do your students account for the popularity of these films.

C. Contribution of Emil Kraepelin: schizophrenia (dementia praecos) and manic depression; each disorder having its syndrome, its course, and so forth.

III. Defining Abnormal Behavior. How do we make the decision that someone's behavior is normal or abnormal? The following criteria are usually used:

A. Infrequent behavior. (Not sufficient: Einstein was a rarity).

B. Socially unacceptable behavior. Pragmatically, if no one is disturbed by behavior, it is not likely to be noticed.

C. Faulty perception or interpretation of reality. It may be useful to define hallucinations and delusions at this time, and to note that we also perceive things differently when we are intoxicated.

D. Dangerous behavior. Persons have been hospitalized because they have been considered a threat to themselves or to others. It is interesting to ask students whether they believe a suicidal individual should be hospitalized against his or her will.

E. Self-defeating behavior. Heavy drinking, phobias, depression, and so on.

F. Personal distress. DSM-III listings of "tobacco use disorder" and "ego-dystonic homosexuality" help make the point.

IV. Different Models or Perspectives for Explaining Abnormal Behavior

A. Medical model: strongly organic, but also includes notion of mental illness (that is, fucntional illness without biological abnormalities). Strong tradition of belief in specific syndromes, courses of illness, dominance of treatment by the medical profession, and so on.

B. Organic model: assumes behavioral abnormalities can be explained by biochemical or physiological abnormalities.

C. Psychoanalytic model: abnormal behavior reflects unconscious conflicts. Medically oriented: symptoms, underlying disorder. Explanations of neurosis and psychosis.

D. Social learning model: stresses that abnormal behaviors are acquired (learned) through same principle of learning that govern acquisition of normal behavior. Stress on situational determinants of behaviors--for example, reinforcement of abnormal operants, observational learning of patient "role" in mental hospital.

E. Sociocultural model: radical, minority view that sees abnormal behavior as one mode or adaptation to an unjust society.

DISCUSSION QUESTIONS

I. In order to demonstrate the way in which lay people use the word "sick" to describe behavior that they do not understand, I usually cite one or two recent instances of criminal behavior and ask students whether they think the criminal's behavior (such as molesting a child) is "sick." I then ask for the reasons why they view the behavior this way. This leads to a full discussion of issues such as the label of "sick" and the frequency of a behavior, the degree to which the behavior is disturbing to others, the degree to which the behavior seems self-defeating, and the degree to which students cannot understand the person's motives.

I usually try to point out that the label "sick" is overused, a catchall category for behaviors the public does not understand. I then note that there is a danger in such labeling in that "sick" people are not usually held responsible for their behavior--they may be excused for missing a test or a day of work and they may make no attempt to change their behavior.

2. It is interesting to elicit views from the class as to why people commit certain bizarre acts. I do so to point out traces of demonistic thinking--that is, the notion that some "thing" got into someone, or that some "force" was at work in someone. What of the expression that someone is not "himself?" Sometimes when a person's behavior seems bizarre, the class tends to attribute that behavior to situational rather than dispositional factors: "I can't imagine what made him do it." It is possible to foreshadow Chapter 11's discussion of attribution theory by noting that there is usually a bias toward attributing other people's behavior to dispositional factors, such as one's personal decision to engage in a certain behavior.

3. After students have become somewhat familiar with the subject matter of the chapter, I like to ask them what a "psycho" is. Sometimes a class is dumbfounded by the question, and sometimes a vigorous argument develops. Some students make the error of citing a television crime show in which a "psycho" was responsible for a series of murders--this, to them, can be evidence.

Here I sometimes get "tough" with the class. If someone cites a TV show's story as "evidence," I ask the class what is wrong with that and sometimes do not allow the discussion to proceed until someone clearly states the error of using a scriptwriter's lay imagination as scientific evidence. I do not leave the discussion until a number of students I call on state clearly that "psycho" is a lay term that has no specific meaning within the science of psychology. Then I ask students to define terms like psychopath and psychotic precisely.

4. Sometimes I will ask the class to differentiate between a sociopath, a psychopath, and an antisocial personality. Students who quickly state that the terms are interchangeable are guilty of having read the book or of having paid attention to a class discussion.

5. A note: I have been interested to find that some students do not understand the concept of "controlling one's own behavior." They may think, for example, that if a person acts aggressively, his or her behavior is not controlled. It must sometimes be repeated patiently that the issue does not involve compliance with social rules, but whether an individual is capable of making and exerting a personal choice as to whether or not to behave aggressively.

MATERIALS FOR STUDENT DISTRIBUTION

Handout 8.1:   A Brainy Marvel Called PET

A TIME magazine report (September 14, 1981) on PET (position emission tomography), which may become used regularly in making psychiatric diagnoses in future years. News items presented in these handouts may be abbreviated versions of the originals, but they have not been otherwise altered. Thus it is advised that instructors read them carefully to determine whether certain statements are scientifically unsound and should thus receive commentary in the classroom.

Handout 8.2:   A Brief Outline of the Diagnostic Categories Included on Axis I and Axis 2 of DSM—III (1980)

This table shows major diagnostic categories of the first two axes of the DSM—III. Instructors may wish to highlight certain categories of their choosing that could not be included in Chapter 8 because of limitations of space. It has been my experience that students are fascinated by Anorexia Nervosa and by Disorders of Impulse Control.

Handout 8.3:   The Temple Fear Survey Inventory

This 100-item fear survey inventory was developed at Temple University and is used by behavior therapists in assessment of phobic disorders. Perhaps I like it because it has a nice round number of items—fitting in neatly with my compulsive tendencies.

Handout 8.4:   Normative Data for the Temple fear Survey Inventory

This handout will permit students to compare their responses to other college students. It also permits an interesting discussion of sex difference in responding.

Handout 8.5:   Symptoms of Depression

This chart of the symptoms of depression suggests that depression has behavioral, emotional, cognitive, and physiological correlates. The term "symptoms" reflects the medical model, of course, so it is possible to indicate to them that the chart could also have been labeled "Signs of Depression" or even "Behaviors Often Linked to a Diagnosis of Depression."

It may be added that in psychotic depression there are also often delusions that go somewhat beyond the "attitudes" listed in the chart—for instance, delusions of having a terminal illness.

Handout 8.6:   A Deadly Feast and Famine

A NEWSWEEK report (March 7, 1983) on anorexia nervosa.

Handout 8.7:   Designer Drugs

A drug update with this excerpt from an article in Science, '85, March issue, p. 60ff.

New synthesized drugs with narcotic effetcs similar to those produced by heroin but with possibly more disastrous side effects are appearing on US streets. A drug must be declared a "controlled substance" before it is illegal. Because underground chemists can keep altering the molecular structure of these so-called designer drugs, they are both lethal and legal.

CHAPTER 9

PSYCHOLOGICAL ASSESSMENT OF PERSONALITY AND INTELLIGENCE

LEARNING OBJECTIVES

_____

After reading this chapter, the student should be able to

1. Explain the difference among aptitude tests, personality inventories, interest inventories, and intelligence tests.
2. Define reliability and validity and explain why psychological tests should be reliable and valid.
3. Define split-half, test-retest, and alternate form reliability.
4. Discuss the nature of correlation coefficients.
5. Differentiate between objective and subjective personality tests.
6. Describe several different formats used for objective tests.
7. Describe and explain the uses of the MMPI, CPI, Rorschach inkblot test and TAT.
8. Explain what is meant by the Barnum effect.
9. Critically evaluate measures of personality and their usage.
10. Discuss how intelligence is defined by lay persons and experts.
11. Explain how intelligence is operationally defined.
12. Explain how the following individuals defined "intelligence": Spearman, Thurstone, and Wechsler.
13. Explain how intelligence tests are standardized and validated.
14. Define the terms IQ, mental age (MA), and deviation IQ.
15. Recount the development of the Stanford Binet Intelligence Scale.
16. Describe the format of the Wechsler intelligence scales.
17. Summarize evidence for and against the proposition that intelligence tests are culturally biased.
18. Discuss the factors involved in creativity and compare creativity to intelligence.
19. Explain Arthur Jensen's views on the determinants of intelligence, and indicate why they are so controversial.
20. Summarize research concerning the inherited and environmental determinants of intelligence.

LECTURE NOTES

Lecture: Intelligence

I. Concepts of Intelligence

A. I usually begin by asking the class what intelligence is. If someone says "An innate ability," I say something like, "So is swallowing." If the class says "learning ability," I ask them to elaborate and to indicate how someone can demonstrate how "much" learning ability someone has.
B. Distinguish between intelligence and achievement, pointing out that intelligence is presumed to permit achievement. I point out the "irony" that all intelligence tests measure achievement on certain tasks at a certain time, although these tasks are often selected to be broadly representative. It

may be helpful to say that some students think of intelligence as a "knob in the head," almost as in phrenology, and assume that people with bigger knobs are more intelligent--but no intelligence tests give us a ruler to measure a knob in the head.

C. Now I distinguish between one-factor and multi-factor theories of intelligence, pointing out that all tasks thought to depend on "intelligence" intercorrelate to some degree.

II. Intelligence Testing

A. It is interesting to ask the class what types of questions or concepts they would include on an intelligence test, and to have them justify their responses. Point out that vocabulary--knowledge of meanings of words--turns out to be a major predictor of general intelligence. Why does the class think this might be so?

B. Distinguish between individual and group tests. Develop the history of the Stanford Binet Intelligence Scale, defining mental age and the derivation of the IW. I point out that "someone's" IQ is someone's score on a test on a given day--not the size of the knob in the person's head!

C. Describe the Wechsler scales, explaining the rationale for having subtests and verbal versus performance IQs. I now show that the formula MA/CA is meaningless for adults, and develop Wechsler's concept of the deviation IQ.

D. In discussing the issue of cultural bias, I point out that the issue remains muddy because culture-free tests do not predict academic success as accurately as culturally biased tests. I stress that important educational and other decisions should not be made on the basis of a test score anyway. There should be interviews, classroom observations, and consultations with teachers, parents, and other professionals before placing a child in a special learning situation.

E. It is useful to take special note of the correlation between IQ scores, academic success and the skills (including verbal abilities) required for successful performance in our high tech/industrial society. This correlation underscores the fact that we are looking at a measure of "degree of fit" as defined by society's values when we are looking at IQ scores. Yet students, particularly prior to coming to college, sometimes feel that school is irrelevant to the tasks they foresee themselves performing in the adult work world. Ask students to discuss the conceptual and verbal skills they think might have been developed through earlier school experience. (You should be aware that this discussion can bring up issues of class and ethnic background. However, once these issues emerge from the conversation, students sometimes understand better the nature of the claim that intelligence tests are biased.)

III. Determinants of Intelligence

A. I review evidence for the genetic hypothesis, concluding that heredity cannot be ruled out as a major determinant of scores children attain on IQ tests. (Again: Heredity does not determine the size of the "knob in the head"-- not that we know of.)

B. I review evidence for the environmental hypothesis and conclude that environmental influences cannot be ruled out as major determinants of scores on IQ tests. (I give the example: If we were to raise a child with excellent genetic potential in a closet, that child may never live up to that potential.)

C. I wind up by indicating that there is no necessary reason that students should think of persons who score higher on intelligence tests as more valuable than persons who score lower. You may wish to give your students a list of occupations and ask which is most socially useful, which most esteemed, and which they assume to require more intelligence. Then ask which they would most like to have as friends. While raising controversial points, it stimulates discussion and may elicit what many critics have assessed as the anti-intellectualism of the U.S. You can then ask if they think that some people may behave less intelligently than they could if they feared social rejection. (Compare this to Matina Horner's study of fear of success in women.)

DISCUSSION QUESTIONS

I. Ask the class to define the concept of intelligence. During the ensuing discussion, I attempt to gradually lead the class to a recognition that one must somehow operationally define intelligence if one is going to measure it.

2. An operational definition of intelligence is: "What is measured by intelligence tests." Why is this definition (a) useful, but (b) unsatisfying? I point out that many people like to have a theoretical understanding of concepts-- they like to relate them to other concepts in an organized, consistent, meaningful manner.

3. The issue of the relationship between intelligence and race is complex and highly emotional. It is made yet more difficult by the fact that so much research data seems in question, or seems to contain such subtle nuances. When I ask the class to summarize research concerning the determinants of intelligence (and race and intelligence), I try to steer them away from simplistic but easily stated and understood answers. I try ot point out that it is more scientifically accurate to say that heredity has not been ruled out as a contributor to intelligence than to say that heredity is the major (or a major) determinant of intelligence. I also point out that all such studies use some sort of performance--for example, on standardized intelligence tests--as the operational definition of intellignce. Thus it becomes more accurate to think in terms of determinants of intelligence test scores, rather than in terms of determinants to the concept of intelligence per se.

4. Ask students about their evaluation of creativity. Do they see this as an important trait? The notion of creativity can be usefully connected with Maslow's concept of self-actualization to offset the commonly held attitude that creativity is an attribute of "artists and other terrestial aliens."

5. In order to illustrate the power of the Barnum effect, I like to read students this personality description and ask them if they feel it applies to them:

> You have a great need for other people to like you and admire you. You have a tendency to be critical of yourself. You have a great deal of unused capacity which you have not turned to your advantage. While you have some personality weaknesses, you are generally able to compensate for them. Your sexual adjustment has presented problems for you. Disciplined and self-controlled outside, you tend to be worrisome and insecure inside. At times

you have serious doubts as to whether you have made the right decision or done the right thing. You prefer a certain amount of change and variety and become dissatisfied when hemmed in by restrictions and limitations. You pride yourself as being an independent thinker and do not accept others' statements without satisfactory proof. You have found it unwise to be too frank in revealing yourself to others. At times you are extroverted, affable, and sociable, while at other times you are introverted, wary and reserved. Some of your aspirations tend to be pretty unrealistic. Security is one of your major goals in life.

This passage was the earliest used in research into "gullibility" among recipients of personality descriptions: B. R. Forer. "The Fallacy of Personal Validation: A Classroom Demonstration of Gullibility," JOURNAL OF ABNORMAL AND SOCIAL PSYCHOLOGY, 1949, 44, 118-123.

Rather than reading the passage to students, it is possible to give them a brief bogus personality questionnaire, and then, a few days later, ask them to rate this "personal report" as being accurate or inaccurate. Regardless of the method you use to demonstrate your point, you may wish to follow up through two avenues of discussion:

(a)   What features of the report help make it universal, or close to universal?
(b)   What does the Barnum effect suggest to us about how astute "fortunetellers" make a living?

MATERIALS FOR STUDENT DISTRIBUTION

Handout 9.1:   A High Grade for Head Start

This NEWSWEEK (October 8, 1979) article highlights some positive findings by Irving Lazar of Cornell University concerning Head Start programs.

Handout 9.2:   Classifications of Mental Retardation

This chart from Bourne and Ekstrand (PSYCHOLOGY: ITS PRINCIPLES AND MEANINGS, Third Edition, New York: Holt, Rinehart and Winston, 1979) will facilitate discussion of varying degrees of mental retardation. An instructor wishing to pursue this topic would do well to distinguish between cultural-familial retardation (which is environmentally-induced and usually mild) and those forms of retardation that are apparently reflective of biological abnormalities. Reference to certain syndromes mentioned in Chapter 2 may help (Down's Syndrome and so forth).

Handout 9.3:   Inventing Gender Differences

In this handout, the heredity/environment controversy is updated with reference to gender differences and abilities in math and science.
Science '85, June, p. 14.

Handout 9.4:   Two Inkblots

My students have always been fascinated by the Rorschach Inkblot Test, and the text contains Card I from the Rorschach.   On a number of occasions I have shown my students the two inkblots on this handout, and asked them, "What could this be? what does this look like?" or "What does this resemble?" They appear to enjoy these two blots, which do not appear on the Rorschach.

Although I have made no effort to obtain scientific normative data for these two inkblots, the following are nontheless some of the apparently "popular" responses they tend to elicit from students:

LEFT BLOT	RIGHT BLOT
Jet plane, seen from above or underneath	Winged human type figure
	Fantastic winged figure
Rocket	Female genital anatomy (external)
Flying animal	Pelvic bone
Crab claws (the projection in front of the "wings")	

I mention to my students that these blots tend to elicit whole (W) responses, and that they tend to project movement (M) into the blots. (Movement means a sense of posture or life as well as displacement of space.)

Handout 9.5:   Behavior Determinants Test

Both heredity and environment--nature and nurture--are determinants of human behavior and personality. This test will permit students to see whether they tend to favor nature or nurture in their own attributions of behavior and personality on issues ranging from intelligence to learning and mothering. The test will take about twenty minutes to administer.

Agreement with the following items indicates attribution of behavior to heredity (nature): 2, 4, 8, 9, 10, 12, 13, 15, 16, 18, 20, 21, 24, 26, 28, 31, 34.

Agreement with the following items indicates attribution of behavior to environmental influences (nurture):   1, 3, 5, 6, 7, 11, 14, 17, 19, 22, 23, 25, 27, 29, 30, 32, 33.

Please note that this test, as a number of other materials for student distribution, may be used in connection with instruction in various chapters. For instance, it would fit in with Chapter 1's discussion of perspective in psychology, with Chapter 4's discussion of learning, and with Chapter 6's discussion of nature versus nurture. It may also be that the instructor will find this test somewhat redundant with the Psychological Viewpoint Questionnaire (Handout 1.3), so that only one would be chosen for class use.

Handout 9.6:   What is Mental Health?   Form A

Handouts 9.7 and 9.8 permit a classroom demonstration of the fact that society has many different expectations for the behavior of mentally healthy men and mentally healthy women. You may find that the class expects the mentally healthy male to behave like a mentally healthy adult, but not the mentally healthy female. This finding would be consistent with the findings of the 1907 Broverman study (Broverman, I.K., Broverman, D.M., Clarkson, F.E., Rosendrantz, P.S., and Vogel, S.R., "Sex-role Stereotypes and Clinical Judgments of Mental Health," JOURNAL OF CONSULTING AND CLININCAL PSYCHOLOGY, 1970, 34, pp. 1-7), in which it was shown that their social perception of the mentally healthy female differed markedly from that of the mentally healthy adult.

For purposes of this demonstration, divide your class into thirds, and assign either Form A, Form B (Handout 9.7, or Form C (Handout 9.8) of the questionnaire to each one of the thirds. Allow about fifteen minutes for completion of the questionnaire, and indicate that results will be anonymous.

After completion randomly collect ten questionnaires from each third--getting an even sex split within groups if possible. You will want to use the ten people sitting closest to the front to help you quickly analyze the results right there in class. Give each of the ten volunteers one of the anonymous Form A questionnaires. Using their help, record on an overhead foil which traits were indicative of adult mental health. To classify, a trait must get 60 percent endorsement. For example, using the ten form A questionnaires (Adult-sex unspecified), if six of ten students indicate aggressiveness as a mentally healthy trait, record it on the foil under the Adult column. If there is a 50/50 split on any trait pair regard that trait as neutral and do not include it. Using your ten volunteers you can quickly read through the pairs asking them to raise their hands as to which of the pairs their questionnaire respondent endorsed. The procedure can then be repeated for Form B (Female), and Form C (Male). By the end you should have recorded on the foil something like this:

Mentally Healthy Adult	Mentally Healthy Female	Mentally Healthy Male
1.	1.	1.
2. List applicable traits here.	2. ditto	2. ditto
3. etc.	3.	3.

By having these lined up in this manner you and your students can readily see the results. Are there any discrepancies? How do the three differ? How do they resemble each other? If there are large differences, get your class to discuss why. How might various definitions of mental health, for example, self-actualization, mastery of the environment, fulfillment of one's potential, adjustment to one's environment, affect our view of a mentally healthy male versus female? Could these call up differences in our perceptions? At this point you might want to discuss briefly the earlier study and its implications for therapy.

Note that the Broverman studies in sex-role stereotypes are discussed in Chapter 3 under the heading of "Social Perception." Some instructors may prefer to use Handouts 9.6 through 9.8 in conjunction with teaching Chapter 3.

Handout 9.7: What is Mental Health? Form B

Please see description under Handout 9.6.

Handout 9.8. What is Mental Health? Form C

Please see description under Handout 9.6.

CHAPTER 10

PSYCHOTHERAPY

LEARNING OBJECTIVES

After reading this chapter the student should be able to:

1. Define psychotherapy.
2. Trace the history of treatment of abnormal behavior from ancient exorcism to asylums, mental hospitals, and the community mental-health movement.
3. Discuss the controversy concerning hospitalization of persons showing abnormal behavoir problems.
4. Describe the educational backgrounds and competencies of various mental-health professionals.
5. Explain the philosophical difference between in-sight oriented psychotherapies and behavior therapies.
6. Explain the goals and treatment methods of psychoanalysis including free association and dream analysis.
7. Explain the role of transference in psychoanalysis.
8. Critically evaluate psychoanalysis as a form of psychotherapy.
9. Explain the goals and treatment methods of client-centered therapy.
10. Critically evaluate client-centered therapy.
11. Describe and evaluate transactional analysis.
12. Describe and evaluate Gestalt therapy.
13. Discuss the controversies over including the category of cognitive therapy. (That is, (1) What is cognitive therapy? (2) Is cognitive therapy insight-oriented)
14. Describe methods of cognitive therapy and evaluate its effectiveness.
15. Describe systematic desensitization and discuss the symptom substitution controversy.
16. Describe aversive conditioning, using the examples of "A Clockwork Orange" and rapid smoking.
17. Describe operant conditioning methods, including the example of the token economy.
18. Describe various methods of assertiveness training.
19. Explain the purposes of, and how one carries out, a functional analysis of behavior.
20. List and provide examples of self-control methods aimed at stimuli that trigger bad habits, problem behaviors themselves, and reinforcements.
21. Discuss the rationales and methods of behavior-oriented sex therapies.
22. Critically evaluate behavior therapy.
23. Explain advantages and disadvantages of group therapy.
24. Describe the goals of encounter groups and family therapy.
25. Describe the use of chemotherapy for anxiety and tension, schizophrenic disorders, major depression, and bipolar affective disorder.
26. Discuss various problems in using chemotherapy. (Side effects? Dependence? Attribution of improvement?)
27. Describe and critically evaluate electroconvulsive therapy (ECT).
28. Describe and critically evaluate psychosurgery.

LECTURE NOTES

Lecture: Behavior Therapy

I. General Considerations in Behavior Therapy

   A. Since psychoanalysis is discussed at length in Chapter 8, I elaborate on the other psychotherapeutic alternatives when I reach this chapter.
   B. Behavior therapy focuses on modifying problem behavior with or without fostering self-insight. (Many behavior therapists discard notions of insight altogether.)
   C. Systematic application of principles of learning to changing problem behaviors: classical conditioning, operant conditioning, observational learning.
   D. Maladaptive behavior is not seen as symptomatic of an underlying disorder; it is the disorder.
   E. Some users of behavior therapy are behaviorists, but psychologists with varying orientations may use behavioral techniques.

II. Systematic Desensitization

   A. For treatment of phobias: goal is to substitute feelings of relaxation for anxiety in presence of fear-inducing stimuli.
   B. Uses deep muscle relaxation (Jacobson's progressive relaxation).
   C. A fear-stimulus hierarchy is constructed, and relaxation is gradually linked to items higher in the hierarchy, as client focuses on symbolic representations (mental images, slides of fear-inducing stimuli.)
   D. Issue: Why does systematic desensitization work? Evidence suggests that systematic desensitization may work through altering client cognitions that stimuli are in fact dreadful, rather than through mechanical counterconditioning or through extinction of fear.
   E. Issue: Does systematic desensitization result in symptom substitution, as feared by some psychoanalysts? (Burden of proof lies with critics.)

III. Aversive Conditioning

   A. Goal: to help break "bad habits" by associating consummatory behaviors (smoking, drinking alcohol, exhibitionism, and so forth) with an aversive stimulus.
   B. An aversive stimulus (for example, an electric shock) is selected and then paired, repeatedly with actual or symbolic consummatory behavior. Thus consummatory behavior (or thoughts about it) come to elicit the CR (anxiety) to the aversive stimulus. The following diagram is a classical conditioning paradigm that I put on the blackboard, using an example of creating an aversion to alcohol through using electric shock:

73

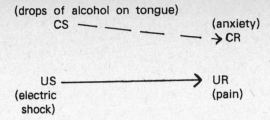

(drops of alcohol on tongue)
CS — —— —— — → CR (anxiety)

US ——————————→ UR
(electric   (pain)
shock)

C. As a result of the above step, an anxiety response can be classically conditioned to alcohol, and may presumably generalize to the thought of alcohol.
Here I say that behaviorists would not use a mentalistic concept like the
"thought" of alcohol, but might refer, instead, to generalization to behaviors
preceding the consummatory behavior itself.
Now, avoidance of alcohol is negatively reinforced. That is, anxiety that
attends drinking, or behaviors preceding drinking, is reduced or eliminated by
avoiding drinking.

D. Students appreciate presentation of examples, such as rapid smoking and
the novel, A CLOCKWORK ORANGE.

IV. Operant Conditioning

A. Therapists encourage clients to emit socially acceptable operants and arrange
for them to be reinforced.
B. Socially unacceptable operants are ignored (not reinforced), and eventually
become extinguished.
C. Example: the token economy.

V. Assertiveness training

A. Distinguish between assertive and aggressive behaviors.
B. Explain use of following elements of treatment in individual and group assertiveness training:
(1) Self-monitoring. I usually mention that self-monitoring of undesired
behavior is often itself sufficient to make dramatic changes of behavior
in people who are highly motivated to change.
(2) Feedback.
(3) Modeling.
(4) Role playing.
(5) Behavior rehearsal.
(6) The broken-record technique.
(7) Fogging.

VI. Self-Control Techniques

A. Goals: to increase frequency of desired behaviors, and decrease frequency
of undesired behaviors.
B. First step: functional analysis in order to identify the situational determinants of behaviors--the stimuli that antecede them, and the reinforcers that
maintain them.
C. Strategies aimed at changing the stimuli that precede behaviors:

(1) Restricting the stimulus field: gradually excluding the behavior from an increasing number of environments.

(2) Avoiding powerful stimuli that trigger habits; examples are very helpful.

(3) Stimulus control: placing oneself in an environment in which a desired behavior is likely to occur (for example, going to the library in order to promote studying).

D. Strategies aimed at changing problem behaviors themselves:

(1) Response prevention: making undesired behaviors difficult or impossible.

(2) Competing responses: using behaviors that are incompatible with undesired behaviors.

(3) Chain breaking: elongating the process of engaging in problem behaviors (for instance, putting a drink down and pausing between sips).

(4) Successive approximations: approaching target behaviors gradually through a series of relatively easy steps.

E. Strategies aimed at reinforcements:

(1) Making rewards contingent on desired behaviors.

(2) Response cost: self-punishment.

(3) The Premack principle: increasing the frequency of a desired behavior by making an already frequent behavior contingent on it.

(4) Covert sensitization.

(5) Covert reinforcement.

VII. Evaluation of Behavior Therapy

A. Helpful in anxiety disorders, problems in interpersonal relationships, some bad habits, and with some patient management problems.

B. Not effective in reducing many severely agitated psychotic behaviors.

C. Not effective in treating "thought disorders" directly (might mention that many behaviorists equate utterances with thought disorder, and claim that decreased psychotic utterances are all that the therapist need seek).

D. Issues: Do behavior therapy methods work because of the laws of learning, or because clients reconceptualize their situations and behaviors while they participate in treatment?

DISCUSSION QUESTIONS

1. What is the difference between a compassionate grandparent (I used to say "grandmother," but was once labeled sexist for doing so) and a psychotherapist? The answer, of course, lies in the definition of psychotherapy—a "systematic interaction" based on psychological principles, and so forth.

2. I usually ask the class to differentiate between psychologists and psychiatrists, and I note that many class members think there is no difference but for the fact that psychiatrists can prescribe drugs and psychologists cannot. Perhaps I become defensive at such terms, but I present my view that psychologists, as a general rule, have many instruments available to aid in defining an individual's psychological problems (that is, tests); psychologists are usually trained to have a more critical view of the psychological theories they may employ; and psychologists may be somewhat more sophisticated in recognition that clinical impressions ought to be supported by data.

However, I try not to speak against psychiatry, since there are many excellent psychiatrists and it may also sound to students as if I am "protesting too much."

75

3. If someone has a psychological problem, how can he or she know what kind of professional to go to and how to find such a professional? This discussion usually leads to criteria for considering hospitalization, for deciding that one should attend one's college or university counseling center, for considering seeing a private psychologist or psychiatrist, and so on. It also leads to a fuller description of types of training of various individuals, and of state regulations for licensing. I point out that students should not be shy about asking about the credentials of individuals they are consulting.

4. In a discussion of laws concerning privileged information and ethics in psychology, I like to ask students what they would do if they were psychologists and a client told them of an intention to commit suicide or to kill another person, or if a minor told them of a relative's sexual abuse of him or her. In such a discussion I refer to the case of TARASOFF V. THE BOARD OF REGENTS OF THE STATE OF CALIFORNIA, during which it was decided that a therapist at a university counseling center was obligated to inform a potential victim of a threat made against her life.

5. Before students have read this chapter, it can be instructive to ask them for their impressions of what happens during psychotherapy. Many students will have the stereotype of the psychoanalyst occasionally saying "mm hmm," or analyzing a dream, or, perhaps, even hypnotizing a client to find out about the past. I point out, in such cases, that certain therapeutic practices occur only in one or a few type(s) of psychotherapy.

6. What are the class's impressions of the people who seek out psychotherapy? Do they perceive such individuals as making mature decisions to seek needed information or help? As weak people who are incapable of making decisions or taking charge of their own lives? As "crazy" people? As spoiled individuals (such as the Hollywood star) participating in a fashionable activity? I usually suggest that individuals have their own reasons for seeking therapy, provide some demographic data on such persons, and say that strong adherence to a stereotype may dissuade some persons from seeing a therapist when they could have profited by so doing.

7. Ask the class if they know anyone (no names, please!) who has received ECT. The student may describe the behavior that led to the ECT and the person's (apparent) response to the ECT. This type of discussion can be extended to other types of biological therapies.

MATERIALS FOR STUDENT DISTRIBUTION

Handout 10.1: Tips on Becoming More Assertive

This handout is adapted from pages 315–320 of ADJUSTMENT AND GROWTH: THE CHALLENGES OF LIFE (Rathus, S. A. and Nevid, J. S. New York: Holt. Rinehart and Winston, 1986). It defines assertive behavior and then provides advice on how students can become more assertive, beginning with self-monitoring of social interactions.

Assertive training, as presented in this handout, is a cognitive-behavioral procedure, attacking irrational beliefs as well as employing principles of operant conditioning in promoting acquisition of assertive social skills.

Handout 10.2:   Using Assertive Behavior to Get a Job

Timely advice from Rathus, S. A. and Nevid, J. S.   BEHAVIOR THERAPY.   New York: Doubleday and Company, 1977.

Handout 10.3:   Cognitive Therapy for Treatment of Depression

In Chapter 8, it was pointed out that recent research by Seligman and his colleagues has shown that depressed individuals are more likely than nondepressed persons to attribute their shortcomings to internal, global, and stable factors.   Ellis suggests that, "neurotic" individuals catastrophize difficulties or setbacks, and Beck has written that the depressed minimize their accomplishments.

This chart taken from ADJUSTMENT AND GROWTH: THE CHALLENGES OF LIFE (Rathus, S.A. and Nevid, J.S.   New York: Holt, Rinehart and Winston, 1986) suggests a cognitive approach to treatment of depression that challenges "irrational" attributions of shortcomings and substitutes more accurate, rational alternatives.   A cognitive therapist might suggest that clients "run a movie" in order to pinpoint self-defeating thoughts.   Then the client would rehearse (practice) the rational thought when appropriate and use self-reward (a mental pat on the back) for thinking the rational alternative.

Handout 10.4:   Some Newspaper Ads for "Therapy"

This potpourri of somewhat flamboyant ads from the New York newspaper the VILLAGE VOICE, indicates the sort of difficulties one might have in seeking "therapy." I discuss the types of "treatment" one might find by following through on these ads, and then develop a discussion of (a) how to find a qualified psychologist, and (b) licensing laws, which, of course, may differ in my state and yours.

CHAPTER 11

SOCIAL PSYCHOLOGY

LEARNING OBJECTIVES

After reading this chapter the student should be able to:

1.   Define social psychology.
2.   Define attitudes and attitude-discrepant behavior, and discuss the relationship between attitudes and behavior.
3.   Discuss ways in which attitudes are acquired.
4.   Discuss research concerning the effectiveness of four factors (the message, the communicator, the context of the message, and the audience) in changing attitudes through persuasion.
5.   Discuss the roles of balance theory in changing attitudes.
6.   Explain the cases of "The Seekers" and Patty Hearst through cognitive dissonance theory.
7.   Define and differentiate between prejudice and discrimination.
8.   Discuss various theoretical approaches to understanding the origins of prejudice.

9. Describe the primacy and recency effects in social perception.
10. Define and differentiate between dispositional and situational attributions.
11. Explain what biases are found in the attribution process. (Students should be able to tie this discussion to the discussion of attributions of failure in Chapter 18).
12. Explain the role of body language (especially touching and eye contact) in social perception.
13. List and describe six factors that contribute to interpersonal attraction.
14. Summarize research concerning the effects of physical attractiveness on social perception.
15. Describe the Milgram studies on obedience to authority.
16. Discuss social facilitation and account for social loafing through the concept of diffusion of responsibility.
17. Define the concepts of diffusion of responsibility and deindividuation.
18. Use the concepts of diffusion of responsibility and deindividuation to explain group decision making (the risky shift), mob behavior, helping behavior and the bystander effect.
19. Describe the Asch studies on conformity.
20. Summarize research on factors influencing conformity.
21. Explain the text's role-playing approach to understanding the concept of romantic love, and why romantic love does not exist in many cultures.
22. Summarize the methodology and findings of the Valins and the Dutton & Aron studies on physiological arousal and feelings of attraction.

LECTURE NOTES

Lecture: Interpersonal Attraction

I. Introductory Considerations

    A. It is possible to begin with a recounting of the story of Candy or Stretch, or to ask the class if they have ever been afraid to disagree with an attractive date for fear of ending the relationship.

    B. I usually define attraction as an attitude that, as other attitudes, involves cognitive, emotional, and behavioral factors.

    C. Then I go into factors influencing attraction.

II. Beauty (Physical Attractiveness)

    A. Some students may think they are "above" being overly influenced by a person's looks, but they usually agree that they will not bother to get to know someone unless there is some physical attraction.

    B. Some studies suggest that beauty is not completely "in the eye of the beholder." I list features rated as attractive in our culture, and mention that attractiveness has correlated positively with overweight in some cultures and that small breasts were valued positively during the American "flapper" era. You may find students interested in the new women body builders. (If possible you may want to see "Pumping Iron II", the film that features many contemporaries in this field.) Women with particularly muscular physiques usually provoke heated discussions.

    C. Advantages of looking good: survey of research into effects of beauty on:
       (1) rating of behavioral attributes (likelihood of being good parent, holding a prestigious job, and so forth).

      (2)   judgments of guilt or innocence in mock jury trials.
      (3)   judgments of talent.
      (4)   expectations of parents, teachers, and other children in school.

   D.   The matching hypothesis:
      (1)   Is a major motivator fear of rejection?
      (2)   Research shows that we usually rate our mates as somewhat more attractive than we are. Why?
      (3)   I elaborate the Harrison and Saeed study, suggesting that a match between beauty and another highly positively valued feature--wealth-- tends to occur through lonely hearts ads.

III. Attitudinal Similarity

   A.   I describe the typical "Coke date" and how social psychologists undertake correlational research that involves measurement of (a) attitudinal similarity, and (b) liking/attraction.
   B.   It is possible to relate cognitive dissonance theory or balance theory to the discussion of the importance of attitudinal similarity.
   C.   Complementarity: Here an individual may be attracted to someone with opposing traits or behavioral tendencies because the interactions will be complementary. The focus is not on attitudes so much as on traits.

IV. The Romeo and Juliet Effect

   A.   Students may recall instances of being attracted to "forbidden fruit." Why do they believe such attraction grows stronger as a result of parental opposition? I mention the possibilities of at least two factors: (1) the adolescent need for independence is heightened by parental opposition, and (2) increased arousal resulting from parental opposition may be attributed to increased attraction to the other person.

V. Reciprocity

   A.   I usually explain reciprocity partly in terms of balance theory: two people each share an attitude toward themselves.
   B.   We are also less likely to fear rejection from someone who expresses an interest in us--that is, we may feel it is safe to make an emotional investment in such a person.

VI. Playing Hard-to-Get

   A.   I recount the Walster experiment.
   B.   Many students have had experiences in which they were "turned on" by a seductive new acquaintance, but were later "turned off" when they observed this person relating to everyone at a gathering in the same manner-- expressing great interest in everyone, hugging, and so on.

VII. Propinquity: Effects of propinquity involve a number of factors, including the following:

   A.   We are more likely to have the opportunity to get to know people who are nearby.
   B.   We are more likely to have things in common with nearby rather than dis-

tant persons. I usually give the example that the boy or girl "next door" is likely to share one's socioeconomic status, and so forth.

C. While affairs with your best friend's spouse always seem most shocking and good soap opera material, propinquity plays a part here. You are more likely to be attracted to friends you spend time with than random strangers.

DISCUSSION QUESTIONS

1. What pressures to conform have students experienced since coming to college? Pressure to conform can be experienced in terms of dress codes, speech patterns, sexual behaviors, political attitudes, traditional family ideology (importance of children, role of the woman, and so forth), and in many other areas of life. Have any students experienced conflict because college students tend to be more socially liberal than are persons in the home environment?

2. What are some of students' favorite or most hated TV commercials? What techniques are these commercials using in an effort or persuade the viewer to use a product? What are the characteristics of the communicators, of the message itself?

3. What appears to determine the friendships that form on campus or in the dorms? Do students become close to their roommates? If so, why? If not, why not? I point out that propinquity plus attitudinal similiarity are a powerful combination in promotion of the formation of a friendship.

4. What are class members looking for in their dating lives? What types of partners are they seeking? Some men and women are seeking partners whom they can look upon as equals in all areas of life. But some male students will be seeking submissive women who have traditional family ideologies. On the other hand, some women will be seeking "strong" men they can respect, and view their educations as "something they can fall back upon," but expect their husbands' "careers" to take precedence over their own "jobs." A class may "jump all over" a traditionally minded student, and they may need a bit of support from the instructor-- in the sense that they are entitled to their views and are seeking what they believe will make them happy, as are other students.

5. It is a dangerous undertaking, but it may be possible to ask class members what stereotypes they harbored about other ethnic groups before they went away to college, and whether these stereotypes have at all changed as a result of the college experience.

6. In another dangerous undertaking, it may be possible to ask students if they "know of anyone who" has done things as a member of a group, such as a "gang," that he or she would probably not have done as an individual.

7. Who determines the seating arrangements when students go out to eat? If a student and a date sit in a booth for four, do they sit next to one another or across from one another? What is their seating preference? Do males prefer to sit across from and females prefer to six next to dates?

8. Students are quite fascinated by the notion that people may have a difficult time differentiating between arousal that stems from a source of danger, as in fear, and an attractive person of the opposite sex--as exemplified by the Dutton and Aron study. They usually have a good time attempting to apply

80

this knowledge to a class discussion of how to create such arousal in dates and then lead one's date to attribute this arousal to sexual attraction. Don't fail to mention the Roman pet Ovid's suggestion to take dates to gladiator contests!

9. Is romantic love an "irrational" emotion? In discussion, bring the class around to recognition that romantic love seems to exist only in cultures that teach and believe in the concept, and that romantic love appears to involve idealization of the loved one.

10. How can you help yourself "fall out of love" if you find yourself enamored of someone you feel is not right for you? The lass is usually enthralled by Ovid's (cognitive-behavioral?!) suggestions for falling out of love--for example, focusing on the loved one's behavioral and physical faults (warts, body odor, and the like) rather than on his or her positive traits, or thinking of the loved one when you are angry about something or in a bad mood for some other reason.

MATERIALS FOR STUDENTS DISTRIBUTION

Handout 11.1:   A Brief Experiment in Social Perception

Do good things come in pretty packages? This brief experiment may demonstrate to your students that they are generally likely to assume that good things are more attractively packaged. If your students are similar to sixty students who participated in a similar experiment at the University of Minnesota (Dion, Berscheid, and Walster, 1972), they probably rated the more physically attractive member of the male and female pairs more favorably on most of the scales. They probably also answered that the more attractive individual would be more likely to feel fulfilled, and less likely to be divorced.

The photos are taken from ADJUSTMENT AND GROWTH: THE CHALLENGES OF LIFE (Rathus, S. A. and Nevid, J. S. New York: Holt, Rinehart and Winston, 1986).

THE WHOLE PSYCHOLOGY CATALOGUE:

A POTPOURRI OF NEWS ITEMS,

ACTIVITIES, PROJECTS, QUESTIONNAIRES,

AND CLASSROOM DEMONSTRATIONS

LOVE STORY

Shutting down Marineland of the Pacific in Palos Verdes, Calif., for renovations two months ago has had a bad effect on some of its aquatic performers. While the walruses have largely kept their cuddly cool, the dolphins and killer whales have shown signs of sorely missing their human audiences. Curator Tom Otten reports that they have become short-tempered, stare balefully at strangers and deliberately make mistakes when doing tricks with their trainers. Says he: "It's like a kid who slams the door, knowing that his mother will ask what's wrong and show him some sympathy." This watery form of anthropomania doubtless is an acquired trait, since in their natural habitat none of the mammals are aware of humans. Indeed, Trainer Tim Desmond suspects that his charges have come to love the roar of the crowds too much. With the park closed, he says, "I think they have become afraid that their livelihood is disappearing."

CUTTING OUT MONKEY BUSINESS
India's Ban on exports perils U.S. medical tests

India's Prime Minister Morarji Desai, 81, is such a devout Hindu that he not only refuses to eat meat but he refuses to be vaccinated against smallpox because cattle were used to make the vaccine. Now Desai has decided to ban the export of rhesus monkeys as of April 1. India is the world's largest exporter of the animals (20,000 last year), and the U.S. is the largest importer (more than 12,000). If Desai's ban takes effect on schedule-- and one aide says the Prime Minister's "mind is closed"--it will jeopardize the process by which polio vaccine and similar products are made and tested. Hundreds of scientific research projects in the U.S. will also be delayed or cancelled.

Desai's personal beliefs can hardly be blamed, however, for the crisis confronting so much research. The chief culprits, according to American as well as Indian sources, are agencies of the U.S. armed forces, particularly the Armed Forces Radiobiology Research Institute (AFRRI). When the U.S. and India first formally regulated the exports of monkeys back in 1955, their agreement specified that for each shipment, the Surgeon General of the U.S. Public Health Service must sign a statement declaring: "I hereby certify that the monkeys now being purchased will be used only for medical research or the production of anti-poliomyelitis vaccine...and that regular inspections shall be made to assure humane treatment of these monkeys." The agreement also declared that rhesus monkeys "will not be used in atomic blast experiments or for space research."

Although U.S. officials deny any violation of that agreement, the Defense Nuclear Agency reports that in five years ending last June, AFRRI used 1,379 primates--undoubtedly nearly all of them rhesus monkeys--in its tests. One typical set of tests was designed to stimulate the effects of the neutron bomb, which kills not by blast or burning but by radiation. In order to determine monkey's work capacity when healthy, they were conditioned by means of electric shocks to run on a treadmill for six hours. Then they were subjected to huge doses of radiation--from, two to ten times what would ordinarily be fatal for most human beings--then put back on the treadmill to see how their capacities had been impaired and how long they survived. They lasted from seven hours to almost six days. In the meantime they suffered the predictable effects of excessive radiation exposure: vomiting, diarrhea, loss of hair.

Though the Indians regarded the military tests as the clearest violation of the agreement limiting experiments to medical research and vaccine production, they cited other experiments in U.S. laboratories as highly questionable:
* Ten monkeys were immersed in water at 90° C. (194° F.) for 15 seconds for an examination of burns.
* Ten monkeys were shot through the head for a study of gunshot wounds.
* Monkeys were operated on without anesthesis so doctors could study shock.

Scattered around the U.S. are scores of biomedical research facilities that use rhesuses for testing the effects of diet, drugs and other chemicals in relation to a wide variety of human diseases, notably cardiovascular disorders and cancer. Two important studies involve examination of the rhesus while it is still in the womb, letting the pregnancy continue and checking hemoglobin changes that occur about the time of birth, which may be significant in relation to sickle-cell anemia.

For these purposes, the rhesus is considered preferable to other monkeys, both because its body mechanisms closely resemble those of humans and because it has been studied so extensively that new results can be measured very precisely.

THE PSYCHOLOGICAL VIEWPOINT QUESTIONNAIRE

Psychologist William R. Miller of the University of New Mexico has constructed a Psychological Viewpoint Questionnaire which you can use to clarify some of your beliefs about human nature. It will also tell you what major psychological theories you are likely to find yourself in sympathy with as you read this chapter.

Read each of the following statements and decide whether you *agree more than disagree or disagree more than agree* with each one. Write an "A" next to those statements with which you agree more than disagree, and write "D" next to those statements with which you disagree more than agree. Express your opinion about <u>every</u> statement even though you may have some trouble deciding in some cases.

1. ____ In attempting to understand human beings one should stick to what can be directly observed and avoid theory or concepts that cannot be seen or observed.

2. ____ Events taking place in the present are systematically linked to events that have occurred in one's past.

3. ____ A specific piece of human behavior cannot be understood without considering the person and his or her life as a whole.

4. ____ People are basically good (as opposed to neutral or evil). If left to a natural state without external controls, they seek health and personal growth while respecting the right of others to do the same.

5. ____ A person's character is largely determined before he or she reaches adulthood. The only changes that one can expect from an adult are relatively small ones, and these occur slowly over long periods of time.

6. ____ General laws of behavior and experience that apply to all people are not very helpful if you want to understand a particular individual.

7. ____ Much behavior, both normal and abnormal, is directed by unconscious impulses and motivations.'

8. ____ Aggression is an inherent and inescapable part of human nature.

9. ____ People are capable of making major and lasting changes in themselves within a relatively brief period of time.

10. ____ Human behavior can be understood as a continuous attempt to increase pleasure and to avoid pain and discomfort.

11. ____ There are no values inherent in human nature or the human condition—only those that are discovered or learned through experience.

12. ____ Learning processes play a major determining role in the formation of personality and human behavior.

13. ____ Events that occur early in life are more important in determining one's adult personality and behavior than are similar events occurring after the person has reached adulthood.

14. ____ Looking inside a person for the causes of behavior (for needs, impulses, motivations, etc.) is probably more misleading than enlightening.

15. ____ The use of scientific experiments is not an appropriate way to try to understand the psychology of human beings.

16. ____ People are neither inherently good nor basically selfish.

17. _____ In order to change a present pattern of behavior, it is important for the person to explore the past, particularly childhood, to find the causes of the behavior.

18. _____ Little or none of what people do is the result of free will. Behavior is controlled by lawful principles, and free choice is an illusion.

19. _____ The therapist who wants to help a person change should not give direct advice or suggestions. Rather the best approach is for the therapist to allow the person to talk and explore his or her feelings without direction or evaluation.

20. _____ A person is free to be what he or she wants to be.

SCORING THE PSYCHOLOGICAL VIEWPOINT QUESTIONNAIRE

Below are twenty items of letters corresponding to the twenty lines of the PVQ. For each item, circle <u>all</u> of the A's in that row if you agreed with the statement or circle <u>all</u> of the D's in that row if you disagreed with the statement.

Item	B	E	H	P
1.	A	A	D	D
2.	A	D	D	A
3.	D	A	A	A
4.	D	D	A	D
5.	D	D	D	A
6.	D	A	A	D
7.	D	D	D	A
8.	D	D	D	A
9.	A	A	A	D
10.	A	D	D	A
11.	A	A	D	D
12.	A	D	D	A
13.	D	D	D	A
14.	A	D	D	D
15.	D	A	D	D
16.	A	A	D	D
17.	D	D	D	A
18.	A	D	D	A
19.	D	A	A	A
20.	D	A	A	D
	-	-	-	-
TOTALS	B	E	H	P

B = Behavioral
E = Existential
H = Humanistic
P = Psychoanalytic

SOME DOMINANT AND RECESSIVE TRAITS

	Dominant Traits	Recessive Characteristics
Eye coloring	Brown eyes Grey, green, hazel Blue	Grey, green, hazel, blue eyes Blue Albino (pink)
Vision	Farsightedness Normal vision Normal sight Normal color vision	Normal vision Nearsightedness Night vision Color blindness

Hair	Dark hair
	Non-red hair
	   (blonde, brunette)
	Curly hair
	Full head of hair
	Widow's peak hairline
		Blonde hair, light hair
		   (red hair)
		Red hair
		Straight hair
		Baldness
		Normal hairline

Facial features	Dimples in cheek Unattached ear lobes "Roman" nose Broad lips	No dimples Attached ear lobes Straight nose Thin lips

Source: Turner and Helms (1979).

COPING WITH EVE'S CURSE
Doctors are finally treating menstrual miseries.

It has many names; period, monthly, that time, my friend. But for many women the most apt description is the curse. For about half of all women of child-bearing age, menstruation is a monthly misery that causes intense physical and mental discomfort. In the U.S. alone, menstrual problems result in the loss of 140 million hours of work a year. Menstrual pain, say Pathologist Laurence Demers of the Milton A. Hershey Medical Center in Hershey, PA., "probably is the most common cause of absence of women from the work force."

Yet despite its impact, menstrual distress rarely has stirred medical interest. Some attribute the neglect to sexist bias by a male-dominated medical establishment. Says Family Practitioner Penny Budoff of the State University of New York at Stony Brook: "Many physicians act as if pain is women's due and getting rid of it is almost sacrilegious." A more basic reason may be that doctors have been unable to explain the link between a bewildering array of physical and psychological problems and a normal physiological event. As a result, women have been urged to cope as best they can with bed rest and aspirin, or they have been labeled neurotics and offered tranquilizers. Says Psychiatrist-Endocrinologist Ronald Norris of Boston's Tufts University School of Medicine: "When there's no obvious injury, physicians tend not to be sympathetic." Neither is the public. According to a poll conducted for Tampax, 22% believe that menstrual pain is psychosomatic.

There are signs, however, of a shift in attitude. It stems in part from studies showing that the gripping pelvic cramps as well as the headaches, backache, nausea and diarrhea suffered by many women during their monthly flow may be caused by prostaglandins. These potent chemicals, produced by the body, help regulate functions such as blood pressure, blood clotting and reproduction. Says Demers: "Some prostaglandins made by the uterus precipitate the contractions that are necessary for menses and labor. But when they're produced in excess, the uterine muscle cramps." Carried through the bloodstream to other parts of the body, the prostaglandins trigger additional discomfort.

Some drugs inhibit prostaglandin production. Oral contraceptives, for example, are effective but inefficient. Says Budoff: "You have to take 21 days' worth of pills for 24 hours worth of relief. And then there are the dangerous side effects" (increased blood pressure, a greater risk of stroke and cardiovascular disease). Aspirin is helpful against mild pain. Most favored today are three drugs used against arthritis: ibuprofen, naproxen sodium and mefenamic acid.

Less understood than menstrual cramps is the premenstrual syndrome. Days or even two weeks before menstrual bleeding begins, many women experience tenderness and swelling of the breasts, migraine headaches, abdominal bloating and acne. They become lethargic, irritable and depressed. Researchers contend that severely distressed women are apt to have accidents, abuse their children or commit suicide or violent crime.

Dr. Katharina Dalton of London's Premenstrual Syndrome Clinic has been investigating the problem for more than a quarter-century. She recently studied three female convicts who repeatedly broke the law and found that their infractions occurred only in the days just before their period. One woman with 26 convictions was well behaved most of the time, recalls Dalton, "but would suddenly burst out with some attention-seeking episode like arson, assault, or even trying to strangle herself." These incidents occurred at intervals of about 29 days. Eventually, the convict's charge was reduced to manslaughter on the ground that she had committed a fatal stabbing when she was experiencing premenstrual syndrome.

Dalton believes the syndrome is tied to a drop in the level of the hormone progesterone before menstruation. Her recommendation: supplements of natural progesterone. Her ideas are controversial, but she has some supporters in the U.S. Among them is Tuft's Norris, who opened the nation's first premenstrual clinic last April in Reading, a Boston suburb. In addition to progesterone, the clinic offers other unconventional remedies such as vitamin B6, biofeedback and hypnosis. Also available are traditional counseling, diuretics, tranquilizers, antidepressants and advice to cut down on salt, caffeine, sweets and alcohol.

The most helpful treatment for many women may lie in a simple acceptance of their complaints. Says Virginia Cassara, who last year cofounded Premenstrual Syndrome Action in Madison, Wis., to provide information to physicians and the public. "You'd be amazed at how much just knowing you're not crazy helps." But clearly educational effort is just beginning. According to the Tampax survey, two-thirds of the public find menstruation an unfit topic for the office or social conversation and one-quarter deem it unacceptable for discussion by the family.

TIME, July 27, 1981

By Anastasia Toufexis. Reported by Janice C. Simpson/New York and Sue Wymelen-berg/Boston

THE MAKING OF A MIGHTY MOUSE

The mice did not exactly roar, but their extra-large size proclaimed the most exciting success of genetic engineering so far. Last week, in the British Science journal Nature, researchers reported they had transplanted growth-hormone genes from rats into mice-and produced six baby mice that were on average 50 percent larger than usual. There is little demand for jumbo mice, of course, but the creatures prove that it is possible to alter animals genetically in important ways. The same process, say the researchers, could create meatier steers, lead to "gene farms" where animals would produce useful human hormones and provide insights into genetic diseases and cancer.

'ON SWITCH': Genetic engineers have been so successful lately that they have filled a menagerie as strange as Dr. Dolittle's: mice with rabbit hemoglobin and flies with unnatural eye color, for example. But this is the first transfer of such an obvious trait-size-from one mammal to another. The latest step across the genetic frontier began with a delicate bit of genesplicing. The gene for growth hormone, isolated from rats by Ronald Evans of the Salk Institute in San Diego, Calif., had to be linked to mouse genes so that the mouse cell would accept it as its own. Only then would the mouse produce rat growth hormone.

To do this, Ralph Brinster of the University of Pennsylvania's School of Veterinary Medicine and Richard Palmiter of the University of Washington took from mice a piece of DNA that switches on adjoining genes. They fused this "on switch" to the rat's growth-hormone gene, repeating a step they had perfected last year. Next, the researchers injected the fused genes into 170 fertilized mouse eggs. Then they placed the doctored eggs into the Fallopian tubes of six foster mouse mothers.

After the normal three-week gestation, 21 baby mice were born and, even at weaning, it was obvious that some were special. Biochemical tests confirmed it: seven babies were born with the gene and it was active in six of them (in one mouse the gene lay dormant). The largest mouse grew 80 percent larger than normal, and even the smallest was 20 percent bigger; on average, the mice grew two or three times faster than siblings without the growth gene. The scientists think they can manipulate growth rate, too, by tinkering with the amount of zinc in the diets of the mice; zinc activates the switch attached to the growth-hormone gene. In fact, some mice had 800 times the normal level of growth hormone.

FACTORIES: Because the foreign gene "took" in so many of the baby mice, the experiment offers hope that similar genetic sleights of hand-could become routine. The gene for prolactin, which directs milk production, is simlar to the growth-hormone gene and could be engineered into dairy cows to increase their output. Since one of the jumbo mice passed on the growth-hormone gene to some of his offspring, other animals should do the same, perhaps establishing a line of genetically superior beasts.

In addition, certain human genes could be injected into large animals; if the genes work in the new surroundings, scientists could harvest bumper crops of substances needed by doctors, such as the clotting factor missing in hemophiliacs. Currently, scientists use bacteria as hormone factories to make insulin and other products. But animals are better because animal cells process hormones as humans do. This is likely to make hormones more effective in human patients. Finally, now that scientists are becoming expert in turning on genes, they may come to understand how nature does it. "That," says Brinster, "will show how the process goes awry to produce congenital abnormalities and cancer."

NEWSWEEK, December 27, 1982 by Sharon Begley

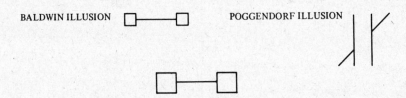

THE DISTORTED ROOM ILLUSION

Which person is larger?

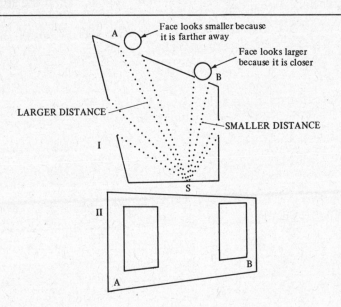

A diagram of the Ames distorted room.

EFFECTS OF POSITVE AND NEGATIVE REINFORCERS

Note that both positive and negative reinforcers strengthen responses and are defined in terms of their effects on behavior. It may be that the examples of negative reinforcers in this figure would be considered punishing by you, but we need not try to guess at your feelings in defining negative reinforcement: we need only note that behavior that is followed by the removal of negative reinforcers is strengthened.

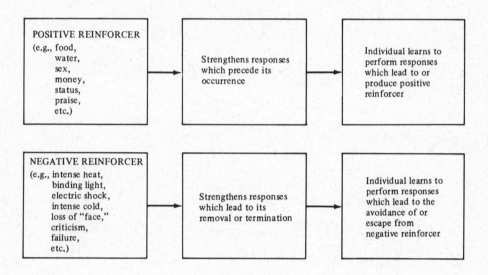

BEHAVIOR PATTERNS RESULTING FROM FOUR INTERMITTENT REINFORCEMENT SCHEDULES

The steeper the lines, the higher the rate of responding.

FIXED-INTERVAL SCHEDULE

CUMULATIVE
FREQUENCY
OF RESPONSES

Total Hours
of Studying

Note long pauses
after each exam

Time ⟶

VARIABLE INTERVAL SCHEDULE

CUMULATIVE
FREQUENCY
OF RESPONSES

Number of Times
Investor Looks
in Mailbox

Note that res-
ponding occurs
at a fairly
constant rate

Time ⟶

FIXED-RATIO SCHEDULE

CUMULATIVE
FREQUENCY
OF RESPONSES

Total Production by
Workers Receiving
Piece-Work Wages

Note brief pauses
after each item
is completed

Time ⟶

VARIABLE-RATIO SCHEDULE

CUMULATIVE
FREQUENCY
OF RESPONSES

Total Number
of Plays on
Slot Machine

Note that there
are no pauses
in responding

Time ⟶

PRINCIPLES FOR USING PUNISHMENT

1. *Avoid inadequate punishment.*

   a. Suspended sentence for juvenile involved in property destruction may encourage further destruction.

   b. Scolding but not making child return shoplifted toy may increase shoplifting tendencies.

   c. Giving just a warning but no ticket for speeding may encourage speeding.

   d. The problem of cheating on exams: _____

   _____

2. *If at all possible, the punishment should suit the crime.*

   a. Convicted drug dealer is required to work in a drug rehabilitation center.

   b. Jaywalker is required to paint all crosswalks in area where caught jaywalking.

   c. Convicted drunken driver must do peer counseling in an alcohol rehabilitation center.

   d. The problem of someone else's term paper being turned in as one's own:

   _____

   _____

3. *At least require an incompatible escape response.*

   a. Vandals' sentence would not be over until they had completely repainted the vandalized house.

   b. Child who throws temper tantrums is not allowed to play with favorite toy 'until an entire day passes with no tantrum.

   c. Embezzler is kept on probation until the amount embezzled has been repaid.

   d. The problem of people who consistently get low grades: _____

   _____

4.   *If at all possible, punish immediately.*

    a.   As soon as puppy urinates on rug, rub its nose in it, spank, and put outside.

    b.   Person giving speeding ticket is required to pay it within 24 hours.

    c.   Child caught shoplifting is required to pay for item immediately out of own allowance.

    d.   The problem of students coming late to class: _____

    _____

5.   *If punishment cannot be delivered immediately, try to reinstate the circumstances.*

    a.   Shoplifting child is required to face the store manager and recount exactly what was done.

    b.   Person convicted of vandalizing a church must return to the church to survey the damage with the church priest.

    c.   Person convicted of reckless driving and injuring someone is required to return to the scene and face the injured person.

    d.   The problem of students plagiarizing: _____

    _____

6.   *Avoid rewards after punishment.*

    a.   Puppy caught chewing up a new shoe should not be fed a snack right away.

    b.   Child told to stay in room for three hours should not be allowed out early to watch favorite TV program.

    c.   Convicted juvenile vandal who is having to pay repair costs out of allowance should not have allowance increased too soon after incident.

    d.   The problem of students who fail an exam and ask what can they do:

    _____

    _____

7. *Always provide an acceptable alternative to the punished response.*

    a. Provide child who likes to hit other children with a rubber doll that can be hit instead.

    b. Juvenile who continues to break windows could be put on demolition crew knocking down old houses.

    c. Dieting person could take up jogging--one cannot eat and jog at same time.

    d. The problem of students with high need achievement who do not do well in school: _____

    _____

A DRUG TO MAKE PEOPLE SMARTER?

The search for a drug to make people smarter sounds almost as futile as the old alchemists' efforts to turn lead into gold. But researchers at the National Institute of Mental Health have made a start: they have found that a chemical in the brain seems to improve memory and learning in both normal people and the victims of depression.

The substance is vasopressin, a hormone secreted by the pituitary gland and long known for its ability to constrict blood vessels and influence kidney functions. The NIMH investigators were inspired to test the chemical as a memory enhancer after encouraging results turned up in animal studies. In their human tests, the researchers used a synthetic drug related to vasopressin called DDAVP. Volunteers got the substance in the form of a nasal spray daily for several weeks. Then they took a variety of memory tests. In one, for example, they were given words that fell into categories, such as fruits, cities and kinds of furniture, and later they were asked to list as many of the words as they could after being told the category. Such ability to recall on cue, rather than simply remember a list of words randomly, is the memory function most important for learning.

DEPRESSION: Young college students scored 20 per cent higher after taking DDAVP than they had on prior tests. A group of middle-aged women suffering from depression showed a 50 per cent improvement in memory, and one-third of them reported substantial relief of their symptoms. Just how the drug accomplishes such changes isn't known. But the investigators suspect that vasopressin and related compounds act on parts of the brain involved in motivation and pleasure, both areas important in the learning process.

DDAVP has some serious side effects; for one, it tends to constrict blood vessels. Thus researchers are now testing similar compounds. If proven safe and effective, such drugs would be especially useful in the treatment of the forgetfulness common among elderly people. They might also be better than coffee for dilatory scholars cramming for final exams.

NEWSWEEK/May 5, 1981

A simple recollection test: Which drawing of the penny is accurate?

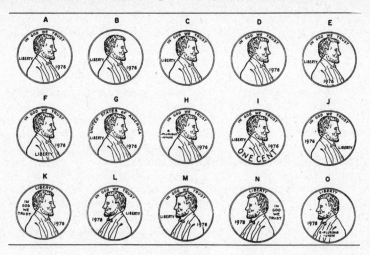

From MEMORY: SURPRISING NEW INSIGHTS INTO HOW WE REMEMBER AND WHY WE FORGET by Elizabeth Loftus.   Published by Addison-Wesley.   Reprinted by permission.

118 pound woman lifts 4,500 pound car

San Diego (AP)--"I don't know how I did it. My body hurts all over now," said 44-year-old Martha Weiss.

Police say the 5-foot-3, 118-pound woman helped rescue a child from beneath a 4,500-pound Cadillac Wednesday by lifting the front end.

"Things like this have happened before," said police spokesman Bill Robinson said, "but I can't recall it being done by anyone so small."

The Tijuana woman reacted after a car went out of control near an elementary school as parents dropped off their children. Eight-year-old Berta Luz Amaral of San Diego was struck by the car and dragged more than 20 feet.

Ms. Weiss said one of the wheels ran over the child and was resting partly atop her when the car came to a stop.

"The mother started screaming" and attempted to pull the child from under the wheel, Ms. Weiss said. At that point, she rushed to the front of the car and begin lifting.

"I could feel the car moving when I was pulling up. I lifted it up enough for the lady to get the little girl out." she said.

Traffic investigators said the woman had grease "all over her from where she had picked up the car. She had tire marks on her slacks."

The child was taken to a nearby hospital, treated and released, police said.

December 6, 1979

THE PLEASANT EVENTS SCHEDULE

What turns you on? Here is a list of 114 activities and events enjoyed by many people. Rate them according to how pleasant you think you would find them by using the scale given below. Then you may want to enrich the quality of your daily life by making sure to fit in some of them.

2   very pleasant
1   pleasant
0   not pleasant

___   1.   Being in the country.
___   2.   Wearing expensive or formal clothes
___   3.   Making contributions to religious, charitable, or political groups.
___   4.   Talking about sports
___   5.   Meeting someone new
___   6.   Going to a rock concert
___   7.   Playing baseball, softball, football, or basketball
___   8.   Planning trips or vacations
___   9.   Buying things for yourself
___ 10.   Being at the beach.
___ 11.   Doing art work (painting, sculpture, drawing, moviemaking, etc.)
___ 12.   Rock climbing or mountaineering.
___ 13.   Reading the Scriptures
___ 14.   Playing golf
___ 15.   Rearranging or redecorating your room or house
___ 16.   Going naked
___ 17.   Going to a sports event
___ 18.   Going to the races.
___ 19.   Reading stories, novels, poems, plays, magazines, newspapers
___ 20.   Going to a bar, tavern, club
___ 21.   Going to lectures or talks
___ 22.   Creating or arranging songs or music
___ 23.   Boating
___ 24.   Restoring antiques, refinishing furniture
___ 25.   Watching TV or listening to the radio
___ 26.   Camping
___ 27.   Working in politics.
___ 28.   Working on machines (cars, bikes, radios, TVs)

___29. Playing cards or board games
___30. Doing puzzles or math games
___31. Having lunch with friends or associates
___32. Playing tennis
___33. Driving long distances
___34. Woodworking, carpentry
___35. Writing stories, novels, poems, plays, articles
___36. Being with animals
___37. Riding in an airplane
___38. Exploring (hiking away from known routes, spelunking, etc.)
___39. Singing
___40. Going to a party
___41. Going to church functions
___42. Playing a musical instrument
___43. Snow skiing, ice skating
___44. Wearing informal clothes, "dressing down"
___45. Acting
___46. Being in the city, downtown
___47. Taking a long, hot bath
___48. Playing pool or billiards
___49. Bowling
___50. Watching wild animals
___51. Gardening, landscaping
___52. Wearing new clothes
___53. Dancing
___54. Sitting or lying in the sun
___55. Riding a motorcycle
___56. Just sitting and thinking
___57. Going to a fair, carnival, circus, zoo, amusement park
___58. Talking about philosophy or religion
___59. Gambling
___60. Listening to sounds of nature
___61. Dating, courting
___62. Having friends come to visit
___63. Going out to visit friends
___64. Giving gifts
___65. Getting messages or backrubs
___66. Photography
___67. Collecting stamps, coins, rocks, etc.
___68. Seeing beautiful scenery
___69. Eating good meals
___70. Improving your health (having teeth fixed, changing diet, having a checkup, etc.)

___ 71. Wrestling or boxing
___ 72. Fishing
___ 73. Going to a health club, sauna
___ 74. Horseback riding
___ 75. Protesting social, political, or environmental conditions
___ 76. Going to the movies
___ 77. Cooking meals
___ 78. Washing your hair
___ 79. Going to a restaurant
___ 80. Using cologne, perfume
___ 81. Getting up early in the morning
___ 82. Writing in a diary
___ 83. Giving massages or backrubs
___ 84. Meditating or doing yoga
___ 85. Doing heavy outdoor work
___ 86. Snowmobiling, dune buggying
___ 87. Being in a body-awareness, encounter, or "rap" group
___ 88. Swimming
___ 89. Running, jogging
___ 90. Walking barefoot
___ 91. Playing Frisbee or catch
___ 92. Doing housework or laundry, cleaning things
___ 93. Listening to music
___ 94. Knitting, crocheting
___ 95. Making love
___ 96. Petting, necking
___ 97. Going to a barber or beautician
___ 98. Being with someone you love.
___ 99. Going to the library
___ 100. Shopping
___ 101. Preparing a new or special dish
___ 102. Watching people
___ 103. Bicycling
___ 104. Writing letters, cards, or notes
___ 105. Talking about politics or public affairs
___ 106. Watching attractive women or men
___ 107. Caring for houseplants.
___ 108. Having coffee, tea, or Coke, etc., with friends
___ 109. Beachcombing
___ 110. Going to auctions, garage sales, etc.
___ 111. Water skiing, surfing, diving
___ 112. Traveling
___ 113. Attending the opera, ballet, or a play
___ 114. Looking at the stars or the moon

Source: Adapted from MacPhillamy, D. J. & Lewinsohn, P.M., Pleasant Events Schedule, Form III-S. University of Oregon, Mimeograph, 1971.

COUNTING CALORIES

Calories Expended in One Hour of Activity as a Function of Body Weight

Activity	Body Weight				
	100 lbs.	125 lbs.	150 lbs.	175 lbs.	200 lbs.
Sleeping	40	50	60	70	80
Sitting quietly	60	75	90	105	120
Standing quietly	70	88	105	123	140
Eating	80	100	120	140	160
Driving, light housework	95	119	143	166	190
Desk work	100	125	150	175	200
Walking slowly	133	167	300	233	267
Walking rapidly	200	250	300	350	400
Swimming	320	400	480	560	640
Running	400	500	600	700	800

What about you? How many calories do you burn up during a day? You can use the approximations given in the above chart to make an estimate. Let's follow Paul, a rather sedentary office worker, through a typical weekday. He takes down his pocket calculator after dinner and jots down his weight: 150 pounds. First he notes that he sleeps about eight hours a night. As we see in the chart below, 8 x 60 (the approximate number of calories a 150-pound person burns up by sleeping for an hour) = 480. Then he notes that he spends about six hours a day at desk work. He eats for about an hour, plus or minus a few minutes, but this is only an estimate. Oh, yes, he drives for perhaps an hour a day. That adds up to sixteen hours.

"Well," he admits to himself, "if the truth be known, I sit quietly for about five hours a day watching television or reading." He works on hobbies (desk work) for another two hours, and exercises by walking rapidly for another hour or so per day. Thus he burns up approximately 2,768 calories in a typical twenty-four-hour day.

Approximate Number of Calories Burned Up by Paul in One Day

Activity	Hours/Day		Calories/Hour		Subtotal
Sleeping	8	x	60	=	480
Desk work	6	x	150	=	900
Driving	1	x	143	=	143
Eating	1	x	120	=	120
Sitting quietly	5	x	105	=	525
Hobbies	2	x	150	=	300
Walking rapidly	1	x	300	=	300
Totals	24				2,768

THREE MORAL DILEMMAS

    1. Recently in Massachusetts, parents of a child with leukemia, Chad Green, were forced into taking their child for painful chemotherapy by the courts. They had wished to treat him with the experimental drug Laetrile and high doses of vitamins. Later it turned out that they were also treating Chad with Laetrile and vitamins, even though the court ordered them to stop because of possible poisoning from these chemicals. Rather than discontinue a treatment they considered essential, Chad's parents took him to Tijuana, Mexico, where he continued to receive Laetrile and vitamins, along with chemotherapy. Chad's parents acted in direct opposition to a court order that prevented them from leaving Massachusetts or directing their son's medical treatment. Legally, they could have been prosecuted for kidnapping. Do you believe they acted morally? Why or why not?

    2. A woman in a Nazi concentration camp during World War II was able to save her family from execution and starvation by having sexual intercourse with the German officers who ran the camp. Do you believe she acted morally? Why or why not?

    3. A moral problem from Kohlberg (163, pp. 18-19): "In Europe a woman was near death . . . There was one drug that the doctors thought might save her . . . (It) was expensive to make, but the druggist was charging ten times what the drug cost him to make . . . The sick woman's husband . . . went to everyone he knew to borrow the money, but he could only get together about . . . half of what it cost . . . So (the husband) got desperate and broke into the (drugstore) to steal the drug for his wife." Do you believe he acted morally? Why or why not?

ATTITUDES TOWARD AGING TEST

Circle T (True) or F (False) for each of the following questions.

T F   1. By age 60 most couples have lost their capacity for satisfying sexual relations.

T F   2. A greater percentage of people over 65 are now working compared to twenty years ago.

T F   3. With advancing age people become more externally oriented, less concerned with self.

T F   4. As individuals age they become less able to adapt satisfactorily to a changing environment.

T F   5. General satisfaction with life tends to decrease with age.

T F   6. As people age they tend to become more homogeneous, i.e., all old people tend to be alike.

T F   7. For the older person having a stable intimate relationship is no longer highly important.

T F   8. The aged are susceptible to a wider variety of psychological dysfunctions than young and middle-aged adults.

T F   9. Most older people are depressed much of the time.

T F   10. Church attendance increases with age.

T F   11. The occupational performance of the older worker is typically less effective than that of the younger adult.

T F   12. Most older people are just not able to learn new skills.

T F   13. When forced to make a decision elderly persons are more cautious and take less risk than younger persons.

T F   14. Compared to younger persons aged people tend to think more about the past than the present or future.

T F   15. Most elderly people are unable to live independently and reside in nursing home-like institutions.

FACTS ON AGING

These facts correspond to each question on the Attitudes toward Aging Test.

1. For most healthy couples the capacity for satisfying sexual relations continues into the 70s and 80s. Important for both sexes is active and frequent sexual expression of some type (Kimmel, p. 216).

2. In 1971 26 percent of men over 65 were working; 46 percent in 1950. For women the percent has remained stable at 10 percent (Kimmel, p. 255).

3. The reverse is true--there is a shift toward increased internalization. Salience of external factors decreases, importance of inner processes increases. There is more concern with one's own emotions and physical functions, an inner-world orientation (Kimmel, pp. 305-306).

4. General adaptive characteristics differ between individuals regardless of age. Little predictable change in adaptational characteristics occurs. Through middle and old age personality traits remain generally consistent and the adaptive interaction between person and social environment remains stable (Kimmel, p. 308).

5. In general there is no noticeable decline in life satisfaction with age. Disease, social losses, and personality characteristics are more important than age in creating dissatisfaction with life (Kimmel, pp. 316, 320).

6. Older people show similar developmental changes just as children, adolescents, etc. do. However, they remain individuals and are not more alike than all young or middle-aged people are alike (Kimmel, p. 317).

7. An intimate relationship--having a confidante to buffer against losses--is highly important for older persons. Depression is less likely, life satisfaction greater for older people with such a relationship (Kimmel, p. 317).

8. Young, middle, and old are all subject to the same range of psychopathology. There is not much difference in incidences of neuroses or psychoses (Kimmel, p. 324).

9. Mild depression occurs in old age as it does at all ages. One study reported only 1/5 of healthy older respondents were rated by psychiatrists as mildly depressed (Kimmel, p. 326).

10. Although no decline in religious beliefs occurs with age, a decline in church attendance does. Possibly religion becomes more internally practiced or a decline in health makes church attendance more difficult (Kimmel, p. 357).

11. Slowed reaction time and impaired ability to master new problems not relevant to past experience are unlikely to affect the average person's occupational performance up to age 60. Because older people are likely to choose situations where experience is valuable rather than development of new approaches, their performance is generally as effective as younger adults (Kimmel, p. 378).

12. For continued learning, health, edcuation, and individual differences are more important than age. Up to 65 there is little decline in learning or memory ability, thus little reason an elderly person cannot learn as well as younger individuals. It may simply take a little longer to learn the same material (Kimmel, p. 381).

13. Although more likely to choose a "no risk" problem solution if available, if not available older subjects take the same amount of risk as younger. If forced to decide, older people are as likely to choose "high risk" solutions as are younger people (Kimmel, p. 383).

14. Older persons do not think more about the past than younger people. Past thoughts are not more prevalent than present or future ones for the aged (Kimmel, p. 414).

15. Most older persons are community residents. At any one time only four to five percent reside in nursing homes (Kimmel, p. 459).

KIDS AND TRAUMA

The child is father to the man: so runs one of the oldest and firmest tenets of psychology, and from it springs much of the conventional wisdom about human development. It's a truism that adult neuroses can be traced to the traumas of infancy, that childhood is a perilous passage in which overprotective or neglectful parents can inflict permanent damage. But recently, because of new studies, some psychologists have begun to challenge this idea with revisionist theories that undercut both developmental psychology and psychotherapy, "You can predict very little (about adult behavior and personality) from experiences at ages 0 to 3, even when they include a number of traumatic events," said psychologist Jerome Kagan of Harvard University last week during the annual meeting in Washington of the American Association for the Advancement of Science.

RESILIENCY: Scientists are discovering that childhood traumas can sometimes be outgrown as easily as baby teeth. For example, only a tiny fraction of battered children grow up to abuse their own offspring; most become normal doting parents. Similarly children who live in orphanages, although often withdrawn, usually become open and trusting once they are adopted and raised in loving homes. Such resiliency, says psychologist Richard Lerner of Pennslyvania State University, "is causing a revolution in our idea of the child."

Perhaps the best clues to whether children can overcome early trauma are found in experiments with rhesus monkeys. One-year-old monkeys raised in isolation behaved much like autistic children; they neither socialized nor communicated with their peers. But when they were put in a cage with normal two- and three-year old monkeys just learning to be sociable, the deprived monkeys "discovered that another monkey could be warm, cuddly and nonthreatening," reports Stephen Suomi of the University of Wisconsin. "As a result, when they grew up, all of their behavior patterns were normal." That discovery might reveal new approaches to human therapy. In one study now under way, psychologists are using 2- and 3-year-old-babies as "therapists" for 4-and 5-year-olds who are mentally or socially retarded.

Disturbing experiences during infancy are more likely to leave permanent scars if they occur in so-called "critical periods." Rhesus monkeys taken from their playmates between their fourth and eighth months, when they learn to interact with peers, become introverted and maladjusted adolescents. Suomi speculates that "mama's boys" sheltered from children their own age when others are learning the socially acceptable limits of temper with both parents and peers often become bullies. Early experience can also bubble to the surface when prodded by similar events later. An 8-year-old child might grieve very little when her father dies, but fall to pieces decades later when her husband dies.

Psychologists studying early childhood experiences are finding some personality traits–like shyness–that seem to persist more than others. In one study, Kagan reported, two-thirds of 21-month-old babies who were afraid of strangers, electric robots and separation from their mothers also acted shy with strangers ten months later. This result suggests that inhibition may have biological roots in the genes or the prenatal environment. Testing this idea, Kagan indeed found physiological signs of shyness. When presented with baffling information, a shy child's heart rate increases slightly and stays high. Normally, heart rate speeds up and slows down as one breathes in and out. After the initial surprise, uninhibited children returned to the normal cycle while inhibited ones retained the elevated rates characteristic of strenuous mental activity. Kagan therefore concludes that biologically shy children are also disposed to be "vigilant," constantly striving to understand the puzzles of their world.

ENVIRONMENT: As psychologists come to understand that infant experiences are less influential than they thought, the new information is bound to challenge traditional psychotherapy. "We overemphasized infancy in the face of disappointments treating problems later in life," admits psychiatrist Robert Emde of the University of Colorado. "It was a matter of thinking that if we understood infancy we could do better." Although the revisionist theory is too new to offer explicit help to troubled adults, one suggestion is that therapists should explore what in an adult's environment has kept an infant experience alive and then try to alter that environment. But probably the most important contribution of the revisionists is the note of optimism they bring to developmental psychology—the notion that apparently permanently ill effects can be reversed by attention and care. The child is less father to the man, it seems, than a visiting relative, only one of many forces that shape the adult.

NEWSWEEK/JANUARY 18, 1982

In Vitro Research

Research off-limits

This is one American medical technology that has grown up backwards. Since the birth of Elizabeth Carr, more than a hundred children have been conceived outside their mothers' wombs in U.S. clinics. But now, say the practitioners of in vitro fertilization, they want to do the basic research needed to support and improve the technique.

A federal moratorium has put this field in an unprecedented state of limbo. In 1975 the former Department of Health, Education, and Welfare announced it would fund no proposal for research on human embryos or on the external fertilization of human eggs unless it was reviewed and approved by its ethics board. That board never approved a single proposal, but before it was dissolved in 1979, its final report concluded that human in vitro research is ethically acceptable, as long as it is applied to solving infertility. Nonetheless, four succeeding secretaries of the department have failed to end the moratorium.

As a result, American in vitro workers have borrowed heavily from investigators in England and Australia. Although American doctors have refined some techniques and improved pregnancy rates on their own, they say it has been slow and difficult work. For one thing, funding must come from patient fees, insurance payments, and private donations--all limited sources. And even those in vitro workers who have collected some private funds are reluctant to directly manipulate embryos. The ban has cast a cloud of suspicion over such experiments, they say.

But if the ban were lifted and the ethical problems relaxed, what kind of research questions would in vitro workers most like to explore?

At the top of everyone's list are experiments that would enable doctors to determine which fertilized eggs have the best chance of developing into a fetus. U.S. doctors now fertilize every viable egg taken from patients and transfer them all back into the uterus. But if doctors could tell which embryos have "the most positive biological intentions," as one researcher put it, they could transfer just a few of these. The rest might be used for research or offered to other infertile couples. Some might also be saved for use by the same woman during a later cycle. Clinical observations suggest the hormones that stimulate development of multiple eggs may make the uterus less receptive to those eggs once they are fertilized and transferred. By saving some embryos and introducing them in a later, unstimulated cycle, doctors say they could increase the odds of a successful pregnancy.

This last option depends on having a way to freeze embryos for long periods, another area that in vitro workers want to explore. So far only three in vitro babies have come from embryos that were frozen and later thawed--all of them in Australia. Although several American clinics are reportedly trying to apply these cryopreservation techniques, others are reluctant because the current method appears to lower some embryos' chances of surviving in the womb.

One of the boldest areas of research suggested by scientists is the detection and repair of defective genes in in vitro embryos. Experiments with embryos might also help researchers understand the working of oncogenes. These are genes thought to perform embryonic functions and normally "turn off" later in life; on occasion, they turn back on and trigger cancer in adults.

The wish lists go on, from mundane experiments to improve the fertilized egg's in vitro culture medium to ambitious hopes of monitoring effects of hormones and drugs by sampling bits of uterus and embryo within a patient.

Gary Hodgen, research director of the Jones Institute for Reproductive Medicine in Norfolk, has something more practical than a wish list. After 15 years of fertility research at the National Institutes of Health, Hodgen quit last year because of the prohibition against human *in vitro* work. Five months ago he landed a $1.5 million research grant from a Massachusetts-based firm.

Hodgen plans to use some of the money to genetically engineer a source of gonadotropins, the hormones used to stimulate follicles. There are now only two sources for these--extracts from cadavers' pituitary glands and urine from pregnant and postmenopausal women. Engineered microorganisms could manufacture the hormones in a purer form and on a large scale, says Hodgen.

Hodgen will also explore the process within the human ovary that causes an egg to mature. And, of course, he plans a series of experiments to learn how to recognize those embryos most likely to survive in the womb. "We will look for a molecular marker released into the spent culture medium," he explains, "either a unique substance or a different amount of some common chemical released by the embryos that survive." Hodgen acknowledges this as a "needle in a haystack approach," but says he wouldn't try any strategy that is invasive, given the current stigma of *in vitro* research.

Hodgen and Howard Jones went to Capitol Hill last year, arguing that doctors are obliged to give the best care to infertile couples, and that the best care depends on basic research. "Couples have a right to have children," says Hodgen. "We don't work against people who have multiple sclerosis or arthritis, and we shouldn't work against people who 'have' infertility."

SCIENCE 85 April, Vol. 6, No. 3, p. 36. Published by the American Association for the Advancement of Science.

The Family Circus reprinted, courtesy of The Register and Tribune Syndicate, Inc.

MEASURING SELF-ACTUALIZATION

For each item, select the alternative that is most like you:

1. a. I prefer to save good things for future use.
    b. i prefer to use good things now.

2. a. My moral values are dictated by society.
    b. My moral values are self-determined.

3. a. I often make my decisions spontaneously.
    b. I seldom make my decisions spontaneously.

4. a. It is important that others accept my point of view.
    b. It is not necessary for others to accept my point of view.

5. a. I try to be sincere but I sometimes fail.
    b. I try to be sincere and I am sincere.

6. a. I have a problem in fusing sex and love.
    b. I have no problem in fusing sex and love.

7. a. People are both good and evil.
    b. People are not both good and evil.

8. a. I find some people who are stupid and uninteresting.
    b. I never find any people who are stupid and uninteresting.

9. a. I am afraid to be tender.
    b. I am not afraid to be tender.

THE <u>ANDRO</u> SCALE: ARE YOU A CHESTY MALE OR A FLUFFY FEMALE?

What about you? Are you, in the words of Stanford University psychologist Sandra Bem, a "chesty" male or a "fluffy" female? that is, do you adhere to strict, traditional sex roles or is psychological androgyny more your style?

To find out, indicate whether the following items from the ANDRO scale are mostly true or mostly false for you. Then use the tables at the end of this activity to compare your answers to those of a national sample of men and women.

Then you may wish to take the test again, answering it as you imagine your parents, brothers, or sisters, or, perhaps, a boyfriend or a girlfriend might answer it. How many chesty males and fluffy females are there in your life?

		True	False
1.	I like to be with people who assume a protective attitude with me.	___	___
2.	I try to control others rather than permit them to control me.	___	___
3.	Surfboard riding would be dangerous for me.	___	___
4.	If I have a problem I like to work it out alone.	___	___
5.	I seldom go out of my way to do something just to make others happy.	___	___
6.	Adventures where I am on my own are a little frightening to me.	___	___
7.	I feel confident when directing the activities of others.	___	___
8.	I will keep working on a problem after others have given up.	___	___
9.	I would not like to be married to a protective person.	___	___
10.	I usually try to share my problems with someone who can help me.	___	___
11.	I don't care if my clothes are unstylish, as long as I like them.	___	___
12.	When I see a new invention, I attempt to find out how it works.	___	___
13.	People like to tell me their troubles because they know I will do everything I can to help them.	___	___
14.	Sometimes I let people push me around so they can feel important.	___	___
15.	I am only very rarely in a position where I feel a need to actively argue for a point of view I hold.	___	___
16.	I dislike people who are always asking me for advice.	___	___
17.	I seek out positions of authority.	___	___
18.	I believe in giving friends lots of help and advice.	___	___
19.	I get little satisfaction from serving others.	___	___
20.	I make certain that I speak softly when I am in a public place.	___	___

21. I am usually the first to offer a helping hand when it is needed. ___ ___
22. When I see someone I know from a distance, I don't go out of my way to say "Hello." ___ ___
23. I would prefer to care for a sick child myself rather than hire a nurse.
24. I prefer not being dependent on anyone for assistance. ___ ___
25. When I am with someone else I do most of the decision-making. ___ ___
26. I don't mind being conspicuous. ___ ___
27. I would never pass up something that sounded like fun just because it was a little hazardous. ___ ___
28. I get a kick out of seeing someone I dislike appear foolish in front of others. ___ ___
29. When someone opposes me on an issue, I usually find myself taking an even stronger stand than I did at first. ___ ___
30. When two persons are arguing, I often settle the argument for them. ___ ___
31. I will not go out of my way to behave in an approved way. ___ ___
32. I am quite independent of the people I know. ___ ___
33. If I were in politics, I would probably be seen as one of the forceful leaders of my party. ___ ___
34. I prefer a quiet, secure life to an adventurous one. ___ ___
35. I prefer to face my problems by myself. ___ ___
36. I try to get others to notice the way I dress. ___ ___
37. When I see someone who looks confused, I usually ask if I can be of any assistance. ___ ___
38. It is unrealistic for me to insist on becoming the best in my field of work all of the time. ___ ___
39. The good opinion of one's friends is one of the chief rewards for living a good life. ___ ___
40. If I get tired while playing a game, I generally stop playing. ___ ___
41. When I see a baby, I often ask to hold him. ___ ___
42. I am quite good at keeping others in line. ___ ___
43. I think it would be best to marry someone who is more mature and less dependent than I. ___ ___
44. I don't want to be away from my family too much. ___ ___
45. Once in a while I enjoy acting as if I were tipsy. ___ ___
46. I feel incapable of handling many situations. ___ ___
47. I delight in feeling unattached. ___ ___
48. I would make a poor judge because I dislike telling others what to do. ___ ___
49. Seeing an old or helpless person makes me feel that I would like to take care of him. ___ ___
50. I usually make decisions without consulting others. ___ ___

51. It doesn't affect me one way or another to see a child being spanked.
52. My goal is to do at least a little bit more than anyone else has done before.
53. To love and be loved is of greatest importance to me.
54. I avoid some hobbies and sports because of their dangerous nature.
55. One of the things which spurs me on to do my best is the realization that I will be praised for my work.
56. People's tears tend to irritate me more than to arouse my sympathy.

Reprinted from Berzins, Welling, & Wetter (1977).

SCORING KEY FOR THE <u>ANDRO</u> SCALE

People who score high on masculinity alone on this scale hold traditionally masculine attitudes, while people who score high on the femininity scale alone hold traditionally feminine ways of relating to the world. Many psycologists now believe that it is possible to experience life more fully and be better adjusted if you score relatively high on both scales. This suggests that you are psychologically androgynous, and can summon up characteristics traditionally attributed to both sexes. That is, you can be assertive but caring, logical but emotionally responsive, strong but gentle.

Your own masculinity and femininity scores are determined by the number of items on each scale you answered in the direction shown on this key.

	Masculinity			Femininity	
Item No.	Key	Score: 1 if same as key, 0 if not	Item No.	Key	Score 0 or 1.
2.	T	_____	1.	T	_____
3.	F	_____	5.	F	_____
4.	T	_____	9.	F	_____
5.	F	_____	13.	T	_____
7.	T	_____	14.	T	_____
8.	T	_____	16.	F	_____
10.	F	_____	18.	T	_____
11.	T	_____	19.	F	_____
12.	T	_____	20.	T	_____
15.	F	_____	21.	T	_____
17.	T	_____	22.	F	_____
25.	T	_____	23.	T	_____
26.	T	_____	24.	F	_____
27.	T	_____	28.	F	_____
29.	T	_____	32.	F	_____
30.	T	_____	36.	T	_____
31.	T	_____	37.	T	_____
33.	T	_____	39.	T	_____
34.	F	_____	41.	T	_____
35.	T	_____	43.	T	_____
38.	F	_____	44.	T	_____
40.	F	_____	45.	T	_____
42.	T	_____	49.	T	_____
46.	F	_____	51.	F	_____
47.	T	_____	53.	T	_____
48.	F	_____	55.	T	_____
50.	T	_____	56.	F	_____
52.	T	_____			
54.	F	_____			

You can use Tables 1 and 2 to compare your masculinity and femininity scores to those of 386 male and 723 female students at the University of Kentucky. Your percentile score (%) means that your score equalled or excelled that of the percentage of students shown. Then turn to Figure 1 to compare your scores with those of people from many different walks of life.

TABLE 1.   Percentile Rankings of Masculinity Scores of College Student Sample

Raw Score	Males (%)	Females (%)	Combined (%)	Raw Score
29	99	99	99	29
28	99	99	99	28
27	99	99	99	27
26	99	99	99	26
25	99	99	99	25
24	96	98	97	24
23	92	96	94	23
22	88	96	92	22
21	80	94	87	21
20	73	93	83	20
19	63	88	75	19
18	54	83	68	18
17	47	78	60	17
16	39	72	56	16
15	30	65	48	15
14	23	58	40	14
13	17	50	33	13
12	13	41	27	12
11	10	34	22	11
10	6	28	17	10
9	4	21	13	9 ·
8	2	16	9	8
7	2	11	6	7
6	1	9	5	6
5	1	5	3	5
4	0	2	1	4
3	0	1	0	3
2	0	0	0	2
1	0	0	0	1
0	0	0	0	2

Total Masculinity
Score: _____
Maximum Score = 29

Total Femininity
Score: _____
Maximum score = 27.

TABLE 2. Percentile Rankings of Femininity Scores of College Student Sample

Raw Score	Males (%)	Females (%)	Combined (%)	Raw Score
27	99	99	99	27
26	99	99	99	26
25	99	99	99	25
24	99	98	99	23
22	99	94	96	22
21	98	87	92	21
20	95	78	86	20
19	91	65	78	19
18	85	53	69	18
17	76	42	59	17
16	65	32	48	16
15	56	24	40	15
14	47	17	32	14
13	37	12	25	13
12	28	6	17	12
11	20	4	12	11
10	14	3	8	10
9	7	2	4	9
8	4	1	3	8
7	3	0	2	7
6	2	0	1	6
5	2	0	1	5
4	1	0	0	4
3	0	0	0	3
2	0	0	0	2
1	0	0	0	1
0	0	0	0	0

A BRAINY MARVEL CALLED PET
New Scanner, a cousin of the CAT, unlocks metabolic secrets.

The latest pictures of the human brain come in electric blues and glowing yellows. They are produced by the PET scanner, one of a series of machines that are helping make diagnosis less of an art and more of a science. The PET scanner looks rather like a sophisticated airplane engine, with a hollow core. It is a cousin of the CAT scanner that nearly a decade ago wedded the technique of X rays with computer technology to give cross-sectional views of internal body structures, not just bones but soft tissues as well. But scanning by CAT (for computerized axial tomography) is limited to anatomy. It lets doctors see an organ's shape and form, but cannot tell how it is functioning. PET (for position emission tomography) allows the physician to examine the brain and body in ways never before possible, providing metabolic portraits, and revealing the rate at which sick and healthy tissues consume biochemicals.

In PET studies, an individual either inhales or is injected with a biochemical; for example glucose, which is the brain's main source of energy, tagged with a telltale radioactive substance that emits positively charged particles. These positrons, when they combine with negatively charged electrons normally found in the body's cells, emit gamma rays that can be detected by a scanning device. Collected and translated into color-coded images, the resulting patterns indicate the intensity of metabolic activity. Because the radioactive substances are so short-lived, anyone undergoing a PET scan is exposed to very little radiation.

PET scans promise to revolutionize certain kinds of diagnosis. Researchers are already using the technique to study blood flow and metabolism in the heart and blood vessels, in hopes of better understanding the mechanisms of heart attacks and strokes and choosing therapy. There is a potential application in cancer as well. Since many malignant tumors consume glucose at much higher rates than surrounding tissue, the efficacy of drug therapy may be measured by the drugs' ability to alter glucose consumption as shown through PET scans.

Still, the most dramatic impact of PET scanning so far has been in studies of the brain. The technique is painlessly providing detailed information about how a normal brain reacts biochemically to such stimuli as the eyes seeing light, the ears hearing a story and even the movement of an arm or a leg. For example, when a subject moves his right hand, the PET scan indicates increased glucose use by the region of the left side of the brain controlling the action. Physicians have begun to use PET scanning in determining therapy for people who have had strokes or epileptic seizures. Measuring metabolic activity in the brains of stroke victims or those with occluded arteries can aid doctors in deciding whether surgery would be beneficial. Scans can also help locate areas of the brain suspected of inducing epileptic seizures.

Some researchers are using PET scans to explore the brains of people suffering from schizophrenia, manic-depressive illness and senile dementia. Their hope is that by scanning hundreds, even thousands, of patients with such conditions, distinctive patterns of biochemical activity will emerge, making diagnosis easier and more precise. Says Chemist Alfred Wolf of Brookhaven National Laboratory on Long Island: "A diagnosis with cognitive tests, for example memory quizzes, takes days. The whole PET procedure takes under 90 minutes."

Preliminary evidence from PET scans suggests that in schizophrenics the frontal part of the brain consumes glucose at a very low rate. In manic-depressives, glucose seems to burn at a very high rate during the manic phase. (No pattern has been found for the depressive phase). People with senile dementia show decreased glucose metabolism; the more advance the case, the lower the activity. Researchers also plan to use PET for biochemical brain portraits of patients with multiple sclerosis, Huntington's chorea and possibly alcoholism.

Presently PET scanning requires highly skilled specialists, including chemists, physicists, mathematicians, computer scientists and physicians. The initial costs are also very high. A cyclotron to make radioactive compounds, PET equipment, and a facility to house the operation can run into millions of dollars. Even so, PET scanners are being set up all over the world. Six years ago, there were only four medical centers in the U.S. where teams of scientists were actively engaged in developing PET. Today there are about ten, including Massachusetts General Hospital in Boston, Washington University in St. Louis, the University of California in Los Angeles and Donner Laboratory at Berkeley. There should be at least 15 different centers involved in PET scanning by 1983. By then Europe will have more than a dozen centers with PET equipment and Japan possibly ten. Says Wolf: "The field is just beginning to take off."

By Anastasia Toufexis
TIME, SEPTEMBER 14, 1981

A BRIEF OUTLINE OF THE DIAGNOSTIC CATEGORIES INCLUDED ON AXIS 1 and
AXIS 2 of DSM-III (January 1979).

Axis 1   Severe Mental Disorders (Including Psychoses and Many "Neuroses")

Disorders That Usually First Mani-
fest Themselves in Infancy, Child-
hood, or Adolescence
  Mental Retardation
  Attention Deficit Disorders
    Hyperactivity
  Conduct Disorders
    Aggressive Conduct Disorder
      Undersocialed Type
      Socialized Type
    Unaggressive Conduct
    Disorder
  Anxiety Disorders
    Separation Anxiety
    Avoidance Disorder
    Over-anxious Disorder
  Other Disorders
    Attachment Disorder
    Schizoid Disorder
    Elective Mutism
    Oppositional Disorder
    Identity Disorder
  Eating Disorders
    Anorexia Nervosa
    Bulimia
    Pica
    Rumination Disorder
    Atypical Eating Disorder
  Stereotyped Movement
  Disorders
      Transient Tics
      Chronic Motor Tics
      Tourette's Disorder
    Other Physical Disorders
      Stuttering
      Functional Enuresis
      Functional Encopresis
      Somnambulism
      Pavor Nocturnus
  Pervasive Developmental
  Disorders
      Infantile Autism
Organic Mental Disorders
  Senile and Pre-senile Dementias
    Multi-infarct dementia
  Substance-Induced Disorders

Alcohol
  Intoxication
  Withdrawal Delirium
  Hallucinosis
  Amnesiac Syndrome
  (Korsakoff Syndrome)
Barbiturates
Opioid
Cocaine
Amphetamine
Hallucinogen
Cannabis
Tobacco
Caffeine
Substance Use Disorders
Schizophrenic Disorders
  Catatonic
  Paranoid
  Undifferentiated
  Residual
Paranoid Disorders
  Paranoia
  Shared Paranoid Disorder
    Folie a Deux
  Atypical Paranoid Disorder
Affective Disorders
  Manic Disorder
    Single Episode
    Recurrent
Depressive Disorder
Bipolar Affective Disorder
Chronic Minor Affective
Disorders
  Cyclothymia
Psychotic Disorders Not Elsewhere
Classified
  Sizophreniform Disorder
  Brief Reactive Psychosis
  Schizoaffective Disorder
Anxiety Disorders
  Phobic Disorders
    Agoraphobia
    Social Phobia
    Simple Phobia
  Panic Disorders
  Obsessive-Compuulsive Disorder
  Post-traumatic stress Disorder

Factitious Disorders
  Factitious Illness with Psycho-
  logical Symptoms
  Chronic Factitious Illness with
  Physical Symptoms
  (Munchausen Syndrome)
Somatoform Disorders
  Somatization Disorder
  Conversion Disorder
  Psychogenic Pain Disorder
  Hypochondriasis
Dissociative Disorders
  Psychogenic Amnesia
  Psychogenic Fugue
  Multiple Personality
  Depersonalization Disorder
  Atypical Dissociative Disorder
Psycho-Sexual Disorders
  Gender Identity Disorders
    Transsexualism
    Gender Identity Disorder of
    Childhood
    Atypical Gender Identity
    Disorder of Adolescence or Adult
    Life
  Paraphilias
    Fetishism
    Transvestism
    Zoophilia
    Pedophilia
    Exhibitionism
    Voyeurism
    Sexual Masochism
    Sexual Sadism
  Psychosexual Dysfunctions
    Inhibited Sexual Desire
    Inhibited Sexual Excitement
    Inhibited Female Orgasm
    Inhibited Male Orgasm
    Premature Ejaculation
    Functional Dyspareunia
    Functional Vaginismus
  Other Psycho-sexual Disorders
    Ego-dystonic Homosexuality

Disorders of Impulse Control Not
Elsewhere Classified
    Pathological Gambling
    Kleptomania
    Pyromania
    Intermittent Explosive Disorder
    Isolated Explosive Disorder
Adjustment Disorders
    with Depressed Mood
    with Anxious Mood
    with Disturbance of Conduct
    With Work (or Academic)
    Inhibition
    With Withdrawal
Other Conditions
    Unspecified Mental Disorder
    (Non-psychotic)
    Psychosomatic Reaction
Conditions Not Attributable to a
Mental Disorder That Are a Focus
of Attention or Treatment
    Malingering
    Borderline Intellectual
    Functioning
    Adult Anti-social Behavior
    Marital Problem
    Parent-Child Problem
    Other Interpersonal Problem
    Academic Problem
    Occupational Problem
    Uncomplicated Problem
    Noncompliance with Medical
    Treatment
    Phase of Life Problem or Other
    Life Circumstance Problem

Axis 2 Personality Disorders (Traits)

Paranoid
Schizoid
Schizotypal
Histrionic
Narcissistic
Anti-social
Borderline
Avoidant
Dependent
Compulsive
Passive-Aggressive
Atypical, Mixed, or Other

Specific Developmental Disorders
    Developmental Reading Disorder
    Developmental Arithmetic Disorder
    Developmental Language Disorder
    Developmental Articulation Disorder
    Atypical Specific Developmental
    Disorder

THE TEMPLE FEAR SURVEY INVENTORY

What do you fear? For each of the following 100 items, write in a number from 1 to 5, according to this code:

1 None
2 Some
3 Much
4 Very Much
5 Terror

_____ 1. Noise of vacuum cleaners
_____ 2. Being cut
_____ 3. Being alone
_____ 4. Speaking before a group
_____ 5. Dead bodies
_____ 6. Loud noises
_____ 7. Being a passenger in a car
_____ 8. Driving a car
_____ 9. Auto accidents
_____ 10. People with deformities
_____ 11. Being in a strange place
_____ 12. Riding a roller coaster
_____ 13. Being in closed places
_____ 14. Thunder
_____ 15. Falling down
_____ 16. One person bullying another
_____ 17. Being bullied by someone
_____ 18. Loud sirens
_____ 19. Doctors
_____ 20. High places
_____ 21. Being teased
_____ 22. Dentists
_____ 23. Cemeteries
_____ 24. Strangers
_____ 25. Being physically as-
        saulted
_____ 26. Failing a test
_____ 27. Not being a success
_____ 28. Losing a job
_____ 29. Making mistakes
_____ 30. Sharp objects (knives,
        razor blades, scissors)
_____ 31. Death
_____ 32. Death of a loved one
_____ 33. Worms
_____ 34. Imaginary creatures
_____ 35. Dark places
_____ 36. Strange dogs
_____ 37. Receiving injections
_____ 38. Seeing other people
        injected

_____ 39. Illness
_____ 40. Angry people
_____ 41. Mice and rats
_____ 42. Fire
_____ 43. Ugly people
_____ 44. Snakes
_____ 45. Lightning
_____ 46. Sudden noises
_____ 47. Swimming alone
_____ 48. Witnessing surgical
        operations
_____ 49. Prospects of a surgical
        operation
_____ 50. Deep water
_____ 51. Dead animals
_____ 52. Blood
_____ 53. Seeing a fight
_____ 54. Being in a fight
_____ 55. Being criticized
_____ 56. Suffocating
_____ 57. Looking foolish
_____ 58. Being a passenger in an
        airplane
_____ 59. Arguing with parents
_____ 60. Meeting someone for the
        first time
_____ 61. Being misunderstood
_____ 62. Crowded places
_____ 63. Being a leader
_____ 64. Losing control
_____ 65. Being with drunks
_____ 66. Being self-conscious
_____ 67. People in authority
_____ 68. People who seem insane
_____ 69. Boating
_____ 70. God
_____ 71. Being with a member of
        the opposite sex
_____ 72. Stinging insects
_____ 73. Crawling insects
_____ 74. Flying insects

_____ 75. Crossing streets
_____ 76. Entering in a room where other people are already seated
_____ 77. Bats
_____ 78. Journeys by train
_____ 79. Journeys by bus
_____ 80. Feeling angry
_____ 81. Dull weather
_____ 82. Large open spaces
_____ 83. Cuts
_____ 84. Tough-looking people
_____ 85. Birds
_____ 86. Being watched while working
_____ 87. Guns

_____ 88. Dirt
_____ 89. Being in an elevator
_____ 90. Parting from friends
_____ 91. Feeling rejected by others
_____ 92. Odors
_____ 93. Feeling disapproved of
_____ 94. Being ignored
_____ 95. Premature heart beats
_____ 96. Nude men
_____ 97. Nude women
_____ 98. Unclean silverware in restaurants
_____ 99. Dirty restrooms
_____ 100. Becoming mentally ill

Fear survey inventory reprinted from Braun, P. R., & D. J. Reynolds, A factor analysis of a 100-item fear survey inventory. Behavior Research and Therapy, 1969, 7, 399-402.

NORMATIVE DATA FOR THE TEMPLE FEAR SURVEY INVENTORY

When you have completed the Temple Fear Survey Inventory, you can compare your responses to those of a sample of 435 students enrolled in an introductory psychology course at Temple University by turning to the normative data in the table that follows.

Normative Data for the Temple Fear Survey Inventory

Item	Mean Score Male	Mean Score Female	Item	Mean Score Male	Mean Score Female	Item	Mean Score Male	Mean Score Female	Item	Mean Score Male	Mean Score Female	Item	Mean Score Male	Mean Score Female
1.	1.1	1.0	21	1.6	1.6	41	1.6	2.6	61	1.7	1.9	81	1.1	1.1
2.	2.2	2.2	22	1.9	2.1	42	1.8	2.7	62	1.4	1.4	82	1.1	1.1
3.	1.5	1.7	23	1.4	1.7	43	1.3	1.3	63	1.5	1.7	83	1.7	1.8
4.	2.4	2.6	24	1.4	1.6	44	2.0	2.8	64	1.7	1.7	84	1.7	2.0
5.	2.0	2.8	25	2.2	3.1	45	1.4	1.9	65	1.7	2.2	85	1.1	1.2
6.	1.5	1.7	26	2.6	2.7	46	1.8	2.1	66	1.9	2.1	86	1.8	1.9
7.	1.3	1.2	27	2.7	2.4	47	1.6	1.8	67	1.4	1.5	87	1.6	2.2
8.	1.2	1.5	28	2.1	2.0	48	1.9	2.7	68	2.1	2.3	88	1.1	1.2
9.	2.5	2.9	29	2.2	2.1	49	2.5	2.7	69	1.3	1.5	89	1.1	1.4
10.	1.5	1.6	30	1.7	1.7	50	1.7	2.1	70	1.6	1.5	90	1.7	1.9
11.	1.6	1.8	31	2.4	2.7	51	1.4	2.0	71	1.4	2.1	91	2.2	2.4
12.	2.0	2.1	32	3.0	3.4	52	1.6	1.8	72	2.0	2.4	92	1.4	1.3
13.	1.5	1.6	33	1.2	1.8	53	1.5	1.9	73	1.7	2.3	93	2.3	2.3
14.	1.1	1.5	34	1.2	1.4	54	2.2	2.6	74	1.6	2.1	94	2.0	2.1
15.	1.6	1.8	35	1.5	2.0	55	2.0	2.1	75	1.1	1.1	95	1.6	1.5
16.	1.7	1.8	36	1.8	2.0	56	2.5	2.6	76	1.6	1.7	96	1.1	1.7
17.	2.0	2.0	37	1.8	1.9	57	2.3	2.3	77	1.9	2.7	97	1.1	1.2
18.	1.3	1.7	38	1.5	1.7	58	1.5	1.7	78	1.1	1.1	98	1.8	1.9
19.	1.5	1.6	39	1.8	1.9	59	1.6	1.6	79	1.1	1.1	99	1.9	2.1
20	2.0	2.1	40	1.7	1.9	60	1.6	1.7	80	1.4	1.4	100	2.1	2.0

These norms are based on a sample of 226 males and female introductory psychology students at Temple University.
Source: Braun (1978).

SYSTEMS OF DEPRESSION

Mood	Behavioral Deficits	Behavioral Excesses	Physical Signs	Attitudes
Feelings dominated by sadness and blueness	Minimal social participation--"I do not like being with people."	Complaints about: Material problems --money, job, housing.	Headaches	Low self-evaluation feelings of failure, inadequacy, helplessness, and powerlessness
Loss of gratification--"I no longer enjoy the things I used to."	Sits alone quietly, stays in bed much of time, does not communicate with others	Material loss-- money, property The demands of others Noise	Sleep disturbances: restless sleep, waking during night, complete wakefulness, early morning awakening	Negative expectation--"Things will always be bad for me."
Professes to have little or no feeling	Memory, inability to concentrate, confusion	Lack of affection from others-- "No one cares about me."	Fatigue--"I get tired for no reason."	Self-blame and self criticism--"People would despise me if they knew me."
Feels constantly fatigued--"Everything is an effort."	Inability to do ordinary work	Being lonely	Gastrointestinal indigestion, constipation, weight loss	Suicidal thoughts-- "I wish I were dead." "I want to kill myself."
	Decreased sexual activity	Expresses feelings of guilt and concern about: Making up wrongs to others	Dizzy spells	
Loss of interest in food, drink, sex, etc.	Slowed speech and gait; monotone speech	Suffering caused to others	Tachycardia	
Feelings of apathy and boredom	Does not attend to grooming; neglect of personal appearance		Chest sensations	
	Lack of joy, humor, delight		Generalized pain	
			Urinary disturbances	

Not assuming re-
sponsibilities
Welfare of family
and friends
Indecisiveness--
"I can't make up my
mind anymore."

Crying, weepy,
screaming

Suicidal behavior--
gestures, attempts

Source: Adapted from P. M. Lewinsohn, Table 1 (p. 23) in M. Hersen, R. M. Eisler, & P. M. Miller (Eds.), *Progress in Behavior Modification*, vol. 1. New York: Academic Press, 1975.

A DEADLY FEAST AND FAMINE

In a grisly way, Americans are by now almost accustomed to the deaths of their beloved rock stars and entertainers from drug abuse. Hendrix, Joplin, Presley, Belushi. But when pop singer Karen Carpenter, 32, died suddenly last month of unexplained heart failure, the reaction was stunned disbelief. By most accounts, Carpenter seldom even took a drink. But like a growing number of other seemingly wholesome young women, she had been abusing her body in a different way. Her addiction: the bizarre, self-imposed form of starvation called anorexia nervosa.

Carpenter, who became obsessed with her weight at least 12 years ago, fits the traditional profile of an anorexic: a talented and ambitious young white woman from a middle-class home. But doctors report they are now also seeing other kinds of patients with food disorders, including a scattering of men, blacks and young children, and many more low-income victims. Anorexia isn't the only such illness. Almost as devastating as bulimia, whose victims gorge on food and then violently purge themselves. Indeed, the diseases—which are closely related—can have disastrous medical consequences. And the lastest research indicates that physiology, as well as psychology, may cause the problem.

ATTENTION: For years anorexia and bulimia were secrets that few victims brought out of the closet, but lately the diseases have gained a certain social respectability that leads more people to seek treatment. Jane Fonda recently admitted to having forced herself to vomit after meals during the early days of her career. And Pat Boone's oldest daughter, Cherry O'Neil, 28 has just written a book, "Starving for Attention," about her grim, 10-year battle with both anorexia and bulimia.

At 16, O'Neil was slightly plump, weighing about 140 pounds. Eager to please her parents and set an example for her three younger sisters, she began to shed weight with extraordinary zeal—and found she couldn't stop. Wearing extra layers of clothing to hide her protruding bones, Cherry exercised six hours a day and stole her mother's diet pills to keep her appetite in check. Eventually she got down to 90 pounds.

Then Cherry's eating habits grew more bizarre. Binging followed by massive doses of laxatives became a relentless pattern, culminating in what she considers her most humiliating moment: Dan O'Neil (now her husband) found her devouring scraps from her family's dinner that had been left in the dog dish. After 10 years of suffering and another disastrous drop to 80 pounds, Cherry finally got psychiatric help and has been able to stabilize her life—and diet. She now weighs 114 pounds. As for her eight-month-old daughter, Brittany, Cherry says: "I want her to feel good about herself as she gets older because of who she is and not how she looks."

MANIPULATIVE: Eating disorders almost invariably disturb familiy relationships, says Dr. Eugene Piazza, director of the anorexia clinic at Children's Hospital Medical Center in Boston. "Siblings get locked out because the whole family is disrupted and controlled by this eating problem." Leslie Gershman, who once plunged to 70 pounds during a long struggle with anorexia, agrees. "It's such a manipulative disease," she admits. "You get people wrapped around your little finger. Any time I wanted my father to visit me in the hospital, I knew he'd be there in a second."

There is no single cause of anorexia. Social pressure on women to be thin plays an important role. A Chicago researcher recently showed that Playboy centerfold models have become thinner every year since the magazine's inception. According to Dr. Nancy Rigotti of Massachusetts General Hospital, 80 percent of adolescent girls have been on a diet by the time they reach 18. But why do some girls and women simply diet, while others literally go crazy over food? Some researchers think the disorders are especially likely to develop when parents set excessively high standards of achievement for their children or try to exert too much control over their lives.

Extreme weight loss can also be a cry for help in a troubled family, or a withdrawal from adult sexuality and responsibilities.

New research suggests that anorexia and bulimia may also have some biological causes. Dr. James Hudson of McLean Hospital in Belmont, Mass., has found that the brain chemistry of some bulimics shows a marked similarity to that of patients with certain forms of depression. When he treated the bulimics with antidepressant drugs, he reports, "the urge to binge seemed to be turned off, much like a faucet." Dr. Michael Ebert, clinical director of the National Institute of Mental Health, has observed changes in the level of certain hormones in the brains of anorexics. Some of the changes are long-lasting, he says, and may explain why the disease is often so difficult to treat.

Obsessive dieting and purging, in combination or separately, take a terrible physical toll. Bulimics develop ulcers, hernias and a dependence on laxatives, and many lose most of their tooth enamel from the acid in vomit. Anorexics nearly always stop menstruating. Their bodies–starved for calories–eventually start feeding on the protein in the muscles. When the heart muscle weakens, it can lead to irregularities in rhythm or even congestive heart failure. Both anorexia and bulimia can destroy the body's delicate balance of electrolytes, particularly potassium, and this can also cause serious cardiac abnormalities.

HEAVY: Anorexia has one of the highest mortality rates of any psychiatric illness. About 2 percent of the victims die, usually due to cardiac abnormalities or suicide. "Anorexics rarely see the dangers," says Craig Johnson, a psychologist at Chicago's Michael Reese Medical Center. "They often insist they never felt better in their lives." One reason anorexics don't realize the risks they face is that most victims vastly overestimate their body size. "A 65–pound person who tells you, 'Gee, I still feel a little heavy, I'd better take off some more weight' is backing off a cliff without knowing it," says Dr. Arnold Andersen, a psychiatrist at Johns Hopkins Medical Center.

Some of the eating rituals are merely eccentric: one young anorexic would chew half a raisin at a time to get two bites out of it. Other behavior is seriously disturbed; some patients have tried to swallow spoons or electric cords to induce vomiting. Barb Robinson, 27 a former anorexic who weighed 85 pounds and thought she might look better at 75, turned to bulimia when she got to college and hit 165 pounds. In the middle of the night she would rummage through the garbage cans in her dormatory looking for half-eaten pizza and submarine sandwiches.

Once an anorexic is willing to get treatment, the most successful approach is a combination of psychological counseling and medical care. Dr. Katherine Halmi, a psychiatrist at Cornell University Medical Center, emphasizes the importance of dealing promptly and directly with destructive eating habits. Some anorexics go through years of psychotherapy while remaining severely malnourished. Being under-weight can cause symptoms like insomnia, irritability and lack of concentration, all of which keep a patient from getting well.

Hospitalization is frequently necessary. At Johns Hopkins, patients spend three months getting round-the-clock medical care as well as psychotherapy. Food is prescribed almost like medicine, with dosages tailored to each patient. The regimen may start at 1,500 calories, gradually build to 4,000 and then taper off to a maintenance level. Fat and milk are carefully rationed since many anorexics have stopped making the enzymes necessary to digest them.

'PIGGING OUT': On college campuses, bulimia may affect as many as 10 percent of the students. Some treat it as if it were the latest fad, "pigging out" and vomiting every weekend–simply for fun. Others are far more seriously affected. To help them, the National Association of Anorexia Nervosa and Associated Disorders (ANAD) has set up chapters on college campuses in 36 states. In New England, a professional theater group is currently touring prep schools and colleges with a show called "FoodFright." Based on two of its actresses' own experiences with eating disorders, the show is billed as "The Hungry Women Cabaret." After each performance the cast joins students and campus health officials for a rap session. The group's simple and comforting message "You are not alone."

Recovery from anorexia can be a long, slow process, and relapses are not uncommon, particularly under stress. But Barb Robinson, who now maintains her weight at 135, believes she is at last finished with compulsive starving, binging and purging. "Everyone is not meant to be thin," she says. "Some women have heavy calves and some are born with a wide behind. As long as they feel healthy, women should forget about trying to look like the models in the magazine ads."

Jean Seligmann with Marsha Zabarsky in Boston, Deborah Witherspoon in New York, Lori Rotenberk in Chicago and Mireya Schmidt in San Francisco

NEWSWEEK/March 7, 1983

DESIGNER DRUGS by Jack Shafer

The new drug was designed to look exactly like heroin. It was diluted with lactose, the milk sugar used to cut heroin, and it was packaged in baloons, just like heroin. It also mimicked heroin's euphoria. When a dealer unveiled it to southern California heroin users in December 1979, he even called the powder China White, the street name for the finest Southeast Asian heroin, and he charged a comparable price. Any confusion between his drug and the real thing was strictly intentional.

The dealer did a brisk business, but three days after Christmas he permanently lost two of his customers, both Orange County men in their thirties. One was discovered comatose in a motel room and ticketed DOA at the hospital; the other died in his bathroom shortly after coming home from work. Heroin paraphernalia – needle, syringe, white powder – was found alongside both men, whose bodies bore the telltale needle marks of heroin mainlining.

Yet when forensic scientists screened the corpses for evidence of narcotic poisoning, they found no trace of heroin. Nor did tests of the white powders and syringe residues found near the victims yield any known drug. "We were frantic," said Robert Cravey, head of toxicology at the Orange County sheriff's office. "Here people were dying after injecting a white powder which looked like lactose to us. We were unable to isolate any active ingredient."

Two and a half years later, a different heroin-like drug struck 42-year-old George Carrillo. He was taken to the Santa Clara Valley Medical Center in San Jose, California, where he lay drooling in his bed, unable to speak. If assisted he could walk slowly but only with a stooped gait. About a week later, his girlfriend Juanita Lopez, 31, entered the hospital suffering rigidness and palsy. Physicians William Langston and Philip Ballard were inclined to diagnose Parkinson's disease, but that neurological disorder afflicts only the elderly.

Carrillo and Lopez's problems had started over the Fourth of July weekend when they shared multiple doses of a powder they called new heroin. After Carrillo injected a dose, he hallucinated, something that had never happened to him before. Within days both suffered stiffness and slurred speech. They were not alone. Two brothers in Watsonville, 50 miles to the south, became paralyzed after they took injections of new heroin.

Since China White's debut in 1979, the drug has killed over 65 heroin users and is now killing at the rate of two a month in California alone. New heroin has given seven users severe brain damage indistinguishable from Parkinson's disease, and more than 200 other users of new heroin may eventually come down with the same paralysis that is crippling George Carrillo.

From the outset researchers knew that both "designer drugs" had been made to look like heroin. They also suspected that both drugs had been synthesized in clandestine laboratories. It wasn't until the drugs were identified that their most important designer feature was revealed: The drugs were completely legal. For until a particular drug is classified as a controlled substance by the state or federal government, that drug remains legal both to make and to use.

China White and new heroin were not the first synthetic drugs to come from a clandestine lab-not by a long shot. Such labs have been illegally synthesizing LSD, PCP, amphetamine, methaqualone (Quaalude), and other drugs since the mid 1960s. Even legal, designer versions of these drugs are not unique. But China White and new heroin did mark the first time anyone had made and sold legal heroin substitutes on a large scale.

As the designer drugs move from their California testing ground to the rest of the country--and there is no reason to believe that they won't--they may well topple America's 70-year-old policy of drug control and spark a public health disaster of overdose deaths, poisonings, and addiction.

From <u>Science 85</u>, March. ⓒ 1985 Science 85. Published by the American Association for the Advancement of Science.

A HIGH GRADE FOR HEAD START

Operation Head Start, the Great Society's heralded pre-school program, has survived budget cutbacks and political skirmishes - and now quietly serves about 390,000 poor children a year. But ever since Head Start began in 1965, its advocates and critics have hotly debated how well it works. Now, a new study directed by Cornell education Prof. Irving Lazar provides persuasive evidence that pre-school training pays remarkable personal and social dividends in later life.

Lazar's team finds "startling differences" between children who attended experimental programs in the '60s and similar low-income children who did not participate. According to the report, the Head Start "graduates" have less need for remedial classes, may have fewer legal problems and are half as likely to become high-school dropouts. The study shows, for example, that the rate of teenage pregnancy did not vary significantly between girls who had attended one Head Start-type program and those who had not; but girls with early educational experiences were far more likely to return to school after their babies were born. Lazar believes that the pre-school programs give the youngsters a more realistic outlook on life. "instead of saying they wanted to be movie queens and baseball stars," he says, "the 17-year-olds wanted to be auto mechanics and beauticians - jobs far above their parents, but not out of reach."

Based on surveys of 2,100 children from low-income families who had been given pre-school training during the '60s, the report concludes that the youngsters benefited from almost any kind of education. The programs seemed of equal value whether conducted in homes, churches or storefronts. And it appeared to make little difference whether parents or professionals conducted the classes. Lazar did not try to measure intelligence. "Head Start's point is not to create geniuses, but to help poor kids keep up with children from more economically advantaged families," Lazar says.

GIL SEWALL with LUCY HOWARD in Washington, Newsweek/October 8, 1979

	Preschool Age 0–5 Maturation and Development	School Age 6–21 Training and Education	Adult 21 and Over Social and Vocational Adequacy
Profound	Gross retardation; minimal capacity for functioning in sensorimotor areas; needs nursing care.	Obvious delays in all areas of development; shows basic emotional responses; may respond to skillful training in use of legs, hands, and jaws; needs close supervision.	May walk, may need nursing care, may have primitive speech; will usually benefit from regular physical activity; incapable of self–maintenance.
Severe	Marked delay in motor development; little or no communication skill; may respond to training in elementary self–help—e.g., self–feeding.	Usually walks, barring specific disability; has some understanding of speech and some response can profit from systematic habit training.	Can conform to daily routines and repetitive activities; needs continuing direction and supervision in protective environment.
Moderate	Noticeable delays in motor development, especially in speech; responds to training in various self–help activities.	Can learn simple communication, elementary health and safety habits and simple manual skills; does not progress in functional reading or arithmetic.	Can perform simple tasks under sheltered conditions; participates in simple recreation; travels alone in familiar places; usually incapable of self–maintenance.
Mild	Often not noticed as retarded by casual observer, but is slower to walk, feed self, and talk than most children.	Can acquire practical skills and useful reading and arithmetic to a 3rd to 6th grade level with special education. Can be guided toward social conformity.	Can usually achieve social and vocational skills adequate to self–maintenance; may need occasional guidance and support when under unusual social or economic stress.

INVENTING GENDER DIFFERENCES

Concocting a biological argument to support a cultural bias is nothing new. At the time of the Immigration Act of 1924, Orientals and Eastern Europeans were considered mentally and morally inferior because of their lower scores on Ellis Island's IQ tests. Arthur Jensen argued only 16 years ago in the *Harvard Educational Review* that inferior genes caused blacks' lower social achievement.

And now, in the 1980s, two Johns Hopkins University psychologists maintain that boys are "born" better at math than girls. As part of a search for precocious young- sters, Camilla P. Benbow and Julian Stanley gave the College Board Scholastic Aptitude Test in mathematics to 10,000 and then, in a second study, to 65,000 gifted 12-year olds. More boys than girls, they found, had high scores. This "male superiority," they stated in a 1980 article, is probably caused by vairables that are endogenous--innate and unchangeable. Women would be better off accepting their differences than to constantly blame their lesser achievement in mathematics solely on social factors, Benbow told a reporter for a science journal. The pair avoided head-on genetic specula- tion in the second study, published in December 1983--"the media has blown this thing out of proportion," Stanley said--but "possible endogenous influences" still crept into a lengthy footnote. They reemphasized their belief that social hypotheses cannot account for sex differences in scores--but still did not say *why* not.

The implication of a spectacular genetic find bedazzled the media. But Harvard population geneticist Richard Lewontin says Benbow and Stanley's notion of the role of gender "came out of their imaginations, not science." The professional educational literature, says Jonathan Beckwith, a Harvard Medical School geneticist, "overwhelm- ingly deals with socialization factors and rarely supports Benbow and Stanley's point of view."

One of Benbow and Stanley's own colleagues in the Johns Hopkins talent search disagrees: Lynn Fox believes that parents are more likely to help boys than girls study for the SAT and that this follows a lifelong pattern. Boys' parents tend to note their sons' math-science interests at an early age, encourage them with math books and Tinker Toys, and plant career aspirations. Girls' parents often overlook, even discour- age, math and science ability. At school, children bend to the stereotyping of their teachers, counselors, and peers. E. W. Haven of the Educational Testing Service, for example, found that 42 percent of girls interested in math-science careers were advised by counselors not to take advanced courses. Other studies show that girls fear being labeled unfeminine if they take math.

The validity of the SAT as a tool for the Benbow-Stanley studies is also open to question. Sheila Tobias, author of *Overcoming Math Anxiety*, finds the studies flawed in their "presumption that the SAT is a test of native mathematical ability, not a test of the man-made conventions of algebra and geometry." The SAT, Lynn Fox recently observed, "has not yet been shown to accurately predict adult creative achievement in mathematics or engineering..."

Then there are the tests conducted by Sharon Senk and Zalman Usiskin of the University of Chicago, which found "no consistent difference between the sexes" on geometry proofs--a reasoning task rarely encountered outside the classroom. "Our data gave a different picture than Benbow and Stanley's," says Senk. "It's categorically not true that boys do better than girls in higher levels of reasoning."

There's no pat explanation for gender differences in math performance--no clean way to unlink genes, hormones, or right-brainedness from social biases. But Senk, assistant professor of mathematics education at Syracuse University, asks, "Even if there were a difference in men's and women's abilities, don't we owe it to everybody in society to encourage them to take as much mathematics as they can for their occupations?"

We think the answer is obvious. Despite all the evidence linking socialization with mathematical achievement. Benbow and Stanley cling to a sorry artifact of another scientific age and reveal their bias: "Girls" don't belong in the male world of math and science.

Robert A. Beckman is a pediatrician at Stanford University Medical Center, Laura Fraser is a free-lance writer.

Science 85, June. © 1985 Science 85. Published by the American Association for the Advancement of Science.

BEHAVIOR DETERMINANTS TEST

For each of the following items, Circle A if you agree with the statement, and circle D if you disagree.

A D   1.   In understanding behavior the emphasis should be on learning rather than biological factors.

A D   2.   Really good newspaper people have an instinct for "where it's happening."

A D   3.   Being raised in an enriched environment can have a positive effect on intelligence.

A D   4.   Understanding behavior can best be done by studying a small number of fundamental building blocks out of which behavior is constructed.

A D   5.   Behavior is primarily shaped through the laws of conditioning.

A D   6.   "Mothering" in humans is a learned behavior, not the result of a maternal instinct.

A D   7.   Learning is more important than instinct for human survival.

A D   8.   Some people are naturally more athletic than others.

A D   9.   There are basic ability differences between the sexes that no amount of training can overcome.

A D   10.   An animal cannot be taught to do things that are extremely dissimilar to what it would instinctively do in its natural environment.

A D   11.   The sum of behavior is more than its individual parts.

A D   12.   We are all born with a collective conscious that helps guide our behavior.

A D   13.   If a child is born of drug addicted parents it is destined to become a drug addict even if not raised by those parents.

A D   14.   Behavior is typically a product of learned wants and needs.

A D   15.   People like professional wine tasters and perfume smellers are born with extraordinary discrimination abilities.

A D   16.   Extremely obese people are born with an unusually strong drive to eat.

A D   17.   Creativity is something you can learn.

A D   18.   One's biological parents are a more important determiner of intelligence than one's "raising" parents.

A D   19.   A good memory is something one develops with practice.

A D 20. Men are naturally more mechanically minded than women.

A D 21. Innate drives such as need for food, sex, and water are more important determiners of human behavior than needs for love, prestige, and money.

A D 22. Your IQ may change as you age; it is not set at birth.

A D 23. Your brain is not a fixed entity; i.e., it can be changed, strengthened, or expanded through learning.

A D 24. The ability to understand mathematics is more instinctively a male than a female trait.

A D 25. Aggression is really a learned behavior rather than a survival instinct.

A D 26. The most important factor in suffering a heart attack is a predisposition toward heart attacks rather than environmental stresses.

A D 27. Personality traits are developed over time; i.e., you are not born to be of a certain personality type.

A D 28. Much of our behavior is controlled by an unconscious, instinctual component of personality.

A D 29. We are not predisposed to be introverted or extroverted; it is a behavior learned through modeling and reinforcement.

A D 30. Women are not naturally more emotional than men.

A D 31. Pathological reactions to today's stresses are most heavily influenced by a predisposition (that runs in families) to react that way.

A D 32. Good coordination is more a learned than an innate ability.

A D 33. The most important determinant of musical talent is one's early environment rather than the specific family into which one is born.

A D 34. Basic psychological urges derive from innate biological needs such as hunger and sex.

WHAT IS MENTAL HEALTH?

FORM A

For each of the following pairs <u>circle</u> the one of each pair which would best describe any mentally healthy adult. Do not include your name. Please do not skip any pairs.

A MENTALLY HEALTHY ADULT WOULD BE:

1.	aggressive	nonaggressive
2.	dependent	independent
3.	unemotional	emotional
4.	tactful	blunt
5.	subjective	objective
6.	easily influenced	not easily influenced
7.	submissive	dominant
8.	gentle	rough
9.	excitable	unexcitable
10.	active	passive
11.	competitive	noncompetitive
12.	illogical	logical
13.	neat	sloppy
14.	home oriented	worldly
15.	indirect	direct
16.	not easily hurt	easily hurt
17.	adventurous	unadventurous
18.	indecisive	decisive
19.	quiet	loud
20.	confident	unconfident
21.	ambitious	unambitious
22.	unassertive	assertive
23.	aware of other's feelings	unaware of other's feelings

WHAT IS MENTAL HEALTH?

FORM B

For each of the following pairs <u>circle</u> the one of each pair which would best describe any mentally healthy <u>female</u>. Do not include your name. Please do not skip any pairs.

A MENTALLY HEALTHY FEMALE WOULD BE:

1.	aggressive	nonaggressive
2.	dependent	independent
3.	unemotional	emotional
4.	tactful	blunt
5.	subjective	objective
6.	easily influenced	not easily influenced
7.	submissive	dominant
8.	gentle	rough
9.	excitable	unexcitable
10.	active	passive
11.	competitive	noncompetitive
12.	illogical	logical
13.	neat	sloppy
14.	home oriented	worldly
15.	indirect	direct
16.	not easily hurt	easily hurt
17.	adventurous	unadventurous
18.	indecisive	decisive
19.	quiet	loud
20.	confident	unconfident
21.	ambitious	unambitious
22.	unassertive	assertive
23.	aware of other's feelings	unaware of other's feelings

WHAT IS MENTAL HEALTH?

FORM C

For each of the following pairs <u>circle</u> the one of each pair which would best describe any mentally healthy <u>male</u>. Do not include your name. Please do not skip any pairs.

A MENTALLY HEALTHY MALE WOULD BE

1.	aggressive	nonaggressive
2.	dependent	independent
3.	unemotional	emotional
4.	tactful	blunt
5.	subjective	objective
6.	easily influenced	not easily influenced
7.	submissive	dominant
8.	gentle	rough
9.	excitable	unexcitable
10.	active	passive
11.	competitive	noncompetitive
12.	illogical	logical
13.	neat	sloppy
14.	home oriented	worldly
15.	indirect	direct
16.	not easily hurt	easily hurt
17.	adventurous	unadventurous
18.	indecisive	decisive
19.	quiet	loud
20.	confident	unconfident
21.	ambitious	unambitious
22.	unassertive	assertive
23.	aware of other's feelings	unaware of other's feelings

TIPS ON BECOMING MORE ASSERTIVE

Assertive behavior involves the expression of your genuine feelings, standing up for your legitimate rights, and refusing the unreasonable requests of others. It also involves withstanding undue social influences, such as pressures to conform and to obey authority figures.

Assertive individuals may also make efforts to influence others to join them in social activities and political actions that they believe to be worthwhile. This may mean becoming involved in political campaigns, consumer groups, conservationist organizations, and a variety of situations that will advance causes they believe in.

Alternatives to assertive behavior include *non assertive* (submissive) *behavior* and aggressive behavior. When we are submissive, our self-esteem plummets. Sometimes failure to express our feelings can lead to smoldering resentments which eventually catch fire and lead to inappropriate, short-lived outbursts. Self-condemnation resulting from outbursts then further lowers our self-esteem. Aggressive behavior includes physical and verbal assaults, threats, insults, and belittling. We sometimes get our way by inducing fear when we act aggressively, but too often we foster the justified condemnation of others. And most of us know when we have been bullies: we are then disapproving of our own behavior, also contributing to lowered self-esteem.

Becoming More Assertive

Perhaps you can't become assertive overnight, but you can certainly decide that you have been nonassertive long enough and construct a personal plan to remake your behavior so that it is more consistent with your genuine feelings. Personal growth takes time and effort.

You might as well face it at once: there may be times when you want to quit and revert to your nonassertive ways. Expressing individual values and personal beliefs may result in conflict—otherwise, we would do it all the time and never have to stand back, take a look at ourselves, and think about it. Often the people we must confront are those who are closest and most meaningful to us: parents, spouses, supervisors at work, close friends.

You can use the following four methods to act more assertively: (1) self-monitoring, (2) coping with irrational beliefs, (3) modeling, and (4) behavioral rehearsal to put your knowledge and your convictions into action.

Self-Monitoring: Following Yourself Around the Block

Very often we are troubled about our relationships. We have vague feelings that something is wrong, but we cannot always put our finger on the problem. You can usually find the source of your problems by following yourself for a while. You may recall that observing the context of our feelings is called a *functional analysis*. Monitoring your social interactions will help you pinpoint your problem areas, and may also help motivate you to take charge of your own relationships.

Self-monitoring is straightforward. Keep a notebook for a week or so and jot down brief descriptions of your social encounters, especially encounters that led to feelings such as anxiety, depression, and anger. For each encounter, note:

* the situation you were in.
* what you felt and said or did.
* what happened as a result of your behavior.
* how you felt as a result of your social interaction.

Below are some examples of self-monitoring taken from Rathus and Nevid (1977). All three people--an office worker, a teacher, and a medical student--were in their twenties.

Jane: Monday, April 6

9:00 A.M. I passed Artie in the hall. I ignored him. He didn't say anything to me. I felt disgusted with myself.

Noon Pat and Kathy asked me to join them for lunch. I felt shaky inside and told them I still had work to do. They said all right, but I think they were fed up with me. I felt miserable, very tight in my stomach.

7:30 P.M. Kathy called and asked me to go clothes shopping with her. I was feeling down, and I said I was busy. She said she was sorry. I don't believe she was sorry--I think she knows I was lying. I hate myself. I feel awful.

Jane's record reveals a pattern of fear that she will not be competent in social interactions and consequent defensive avoidance. But her avoidance has short-lived benefits because of her loneliness, depression, and feelings of self-disgust.

Michael: Wednesday, December 17

8:30 A.M. The kids were noisy in homeroom. I got very angry and screamed my head off at them. They quieted down, but looked at each other as if I were crazy. My face felt red and hot, and my stomach was in a knot. I found myself wondering what I was doing.

4:00 P.M. I was driving home from school. Some guy cut me off. I followed him closely for two blocks, leaning on my horn but praying he wouldn't stop and get out of his car. He didn't. I felt shaky as hell and thought someday I was going to get myself killed. I had to pull over and wait for the shakes to pass before I could drive again.

8:00 P.M. I was writing lesson plans for tomorrow. Mom came into the room and started crying--Dad was out drinking again. I yelled it was her problem. If she didn't like his drinking, she should divorce him. She cried harder and ran out. I felt pain through my chest. I felt drained and hopeless.

Michael was behaving aggressively, not assertively. Pinpointing the behavior that led to higher blood pressure and many painful bodily sensations helped him realize how he was living with many ongoing frustrations rather than making decisions and acting assertively.

Leslie was a third-year medical student whose husband was a professor of art and archaeology:

Leslie: Tuesday, October 5

10:00 A.M. I was discussing specialization interests with class-mates, I mentioned my interest in surgery. Paul smirked and said, "Shouldn't you be going into pediatrics or family practice?" I said nothing, playing the game of ignoring him, but I felt sick and weak inside. I was wondering if I'd ever get through a residency in surgery if every doctor I worked with thought I should be in a less pressured or more "feminine" branch of medicine.

Thursday, October 7

7:30   P.M.   I had studying to do but was washing the dinner dishes, as per usual. Tom was reading the paper. I wanted to scream there was no reason I should be doing the dishes just because I was the woman. I'd worked harder than day than Tom, my career was just as important as his, and I had homework to do. But I said nothing. I felt symptoms of anxiety or anger, I don't know which. My face was hot and flushed. My heart rate was rapid. I was sweating.

Leslie's case was typical. Men did not consider her accomplishments to be as significant as their own, even though she was competing successfully in medical school. It never occurred to Tom that he could help her with the dishes, or that they could rotate responsibility for such household tasks. Leslie resolved she must learn to speak out--to prevent male students from taunting her and to enlist Tom's cooperation around the house.

Coping with Irrational Beliefs: "That Can't be *My* Attitude"

When you are following yourself around, try your best to listen to your conversations with yourself. Ferret out the attitudes and beliefs that lie between the social situations you find yourself in and your responses to them. Our attitudes and beliefs can become so ingrained that we no longer pay attention to them. By not paying attention, we lose the opportunity to reevalute or update our beliefs about ourselves and our relationships with other people.

Jane was avoiding other people because of anxiety concerning her ability to relate to them successfully. She had several irrational beliefs that heightened this anxiety: She believed that she must be perfectly competent in her social interactions, or else she should avoid them. She believed that she was naturally shy, that her heredity and her childhood experiences had forged an unchangeable adult personality. She believed that it would be so difficult for her to act more assertively that she should settle for whatever pleasures she could obtain from life without exposing herself to social stresses.

Many of Michael's frustrations stemmed from a belief that life was somehow unfair to him. He behaved as though he felt people were being purposefully obstinate. People, perhaps, ought to anticipate his needs and try to fulfill them. He should not really have to find it necessary to take charge of his own feelings and his own relationships.

Leslie was quiet about her feelings because of her own failure to tell herself, loudly and clearly, that it was perfectly all right for her to pursue a career that had been traditionally reserved for men, and that it was also all right to expect her husband to assume some of the chores that had been traditionally reserved for women. She had been attempting just to slide by quietly, without making a fuss. Why? Perhaps she had been overly concerned that she might earn the disapproval of others. Perhaps she felt she could not live with such disapproval. Nonassertive people are typically more concerned than assertive people that others will disapprove of them if they express their true feelings (Schwartz & Gottman 1976).

Try to ferret out your own attitudes and beliefs by becoming more aware of your thought processes as you reflect upon your diary. Check the thoughts of Jane, Michael, and Leslie. Could any of them belong to you?

Once you have outlined the beliefs that may be preventing you from expressing your true feelings, the procedure is very simple. Challenge them. Ask yourself if you are utterly overwhelmed by the power of their logic. Will the roof really cave in if someone disapproves of you? Will the Ice Age be upon us next week if you attempt to speak up and flub it once or twice: Will the gods really flit down from Mt. Olympus and strike you down with lighting if you should happen to question an authority figure who makes an unreasonable demand?

Modeling: Creating the New (Well, _Almost_ New) You

Much of our behavior is modeled after that of people whom we respect and admire, people who appear capable of coping with problems and situations that pose some difficulty for us. Kevin Bacon in "Footloose" was a perfect model if you happen to have recently become the "new kid" at the local high school and Jennifer Beal in "Flashdance" became a perfect example for the young woman who saw herself as independent and with great aspirations and without environmental resources.

Therapists who train clients to behave more assertively use extensive modeling. They "model" or provide an example of a way to say something, a way to hold your head or to look the other fellow in the eye as you speak. Then you try it out. The therapist then gives you feedback--tells you how well you did.

Modeling is very useful when you are not certain how to go about acting assertively. Can simply watching characters on television and in films better your own individual style? If so, try that behavior pattern on for size. If you wear it for a while and it fits you well, you may swear that you were born with it.

Behavior Rehearsal: Practice Makes Much Better

After you have decided on making changes, and even given the new you a few lines to say, try them out a few times in a nonthreatening situation rather than immediately confronting others. This is behavior rehearsal. It will help you get used to the sounds of your assertive talk as they come from your own throat. You won't find them shocking and new in the real-life situation.

Assertiveness trainers well know the value of behavior rehearsal. In individual and group sessions, they encourage clients to try out assertive behavior. The trainers may also use role playing: they may act the parts of social antagonists, or they may encourage you and other group members to act out the roles of the important people in your lives. They alert you to your bodily posture, your tone of voice, and your possible problems in maintaining eye contact as well as to the actual content of what you are saying.

The following is a case taken from Rathus and Nevid (1977). Joan was a recently divorced secretary in her twenties. She returned home to live with her parents for financial reasons and emotional support. Six months later, her father died. Her mother, in her fifties, underwent a normal period of grief and mourning. Joan offered all the support she could. But as time passed--three, four, six months--Joan came to believe that her mother was now overly dependent on her. She would not go anywhere by herself, not even drive to the market for food. Joan had come to feel that she must somehow persuade her mother to begin to rely on herself again.

Joan explained her situation in an assertiveness-training group. The therapist asked a group member to play the role of Joan's mother, and Joan rehearsed responding to many possible requests her mother might make. The goal was to refuse to help her mother in such a manner that the mother would eventually see that Joan was interested in her welfare. Joan used the techniques of fogging and the *broken record*. She showed that she understood her mother's feelings, but continued to repeat her basic position. Here is a sample dialogue that occurred in behavior rehearsal:

Mother Role: Dear, would you take me over to the market?

Joan: Sorry, Mom, it's been a long day. Why don't you drive yourself?

Mother Role: You know I haven't been able to get behind the wheel of that car since Dad passed away.

Joan: I know it's been hard for you to get going again (fogging), but it's been a long day (broken record) and you've got to get started doing these things sometime.

Mother Role: You know that if I could do this for myself, I would.

Joan: I know you believe that (fogging), but I'm not doing you any favor by constantly driving you around. You've got to get started sometime (broken record).

Mother Role: I don't think you understand how I feel. (At this point the group member playing the mother role has been instructed to begin to cry.)

Joan: You can say that, but I think I really do understand how awful you feel (fogging). But I'm thinking of your welfare more than my own, and I'm simply not doing you a favor by driving you everywhere (broken record).

Mother Role: But we need a few things.

Joan: No, Mother, I won't be doing you any favor by taking you (broken record).

Mother Role: Does that mean you've decided not to help?

Joan: It means that I'm thinking of your welfare as well as my own, and I'm not doing you any favor by taking you everywhere. You have to start sometime (broken record).

Joan's task was not easy, but eventually she and her mother reached a workable compromise. Joan agreed to accompany her mother for a while as the older woman drove. Then her mother would have to begin to drive herself.

It is sometimes possible to enlist the aid of trusted relatives and friends in role playing when you decide to become more assertive. They can give you valuable information, or feedback, concerning the effectiveness of your words as well as your style of delivery. It is also important to overcome perfectionist self-demands. You will probably make some errors. Accept this. We often learn from our errors as well as from our successes. And at least you will have the comfort of knowing you are striving positively to grow and to take charge of your own relationships.

USING ASSERTIVE BEHAVIOR TO DO A JOB

One of the more critical situations in which you may find it helpful to assert yourself is the job interview. If this prospect is distressing, you can built up to it step by step, through a hierarchy of experiences that involves gradual approach and behavior rehearsal. Early successes have a way of making later goals appear less frightening.

You can break down job-seeking skills into an easy practice level, a medium practice level, and the target behavior level or actual interview:

Easy Practice Level

Read through the advertisements in newspapers. Select several positions in which you have no interest. Call the prospective employer, introduce yourself by name, indicate how you learned of the opening, request a fuller job description than the one offered in the paper, and ask for a fuller description of the qualifications desired in applicants. Thank the employer for his time, and indicate that you will get in touch if you wish to pursue application. You may also wish to ask why the position has become available-- through expansion, reshuffling of personnel, or employee resignation--and for information about the criteria used to determine raises and promotions.

Contact a number of friends and ask them if they are aware of any openings in your field.

Make a list of the assets and liabilities you would bring to a new job. List reliability and concern that a job gets done properly among your assets. Nonassertive people commonly have a blind spot for the value of these qualities in themselves.

Answer a newspaper advertisement for a job in which you might be interested by letter (unless telephoning is required).

Medium Practice Level

Go to your state employment office or list yourself with personnel agencies. Inform these agencies of your assets and of your preferred working conditions.

Use behavior rehearsal to practice an interview with a prospective employer. Write down a list of questions that you are likely to be asked. Include challenging questions such as why you are contemplating leaving your present position or why you are out of work. Expect to be asked what special talents or qualifications you can bring to the job. Look in the mirror and and answer these questions. Maintain direct eye contact with yourself. Rehearse several statements that you will probably be able to use intact, attending to your tone of voice and bodily posture. Have a family member or confidant provide you with social feedback. Use someone who can be constructively critical, not someone who thinks that all your behavior is either perfect or beyond salvation.

Go to local businesses in person, ask for application forms, fill them out, and return them.

Write or, if possible, phone employers advertising openings in which you do have interest. Request a fuller job description by saying something like, "I wonder if you can tell me more about the opening." Indicate that you will send a resume, as required, and that you look forward to the prospect of an interview.

Target Behavior Level

After you have sent in a resume in response to an advertisement and waited for a reasonable period of time, phone the prospective employer and say, "I wonder if there is anything you can share with me about the recruitement process."

During interviews, be certain that you have had an opportunity to point out your assets for the position. Maintain direct eye contact with the interviewer. Admit freely and openly to liabilities that would become evident with the passage of time—such as lack of administrative experience in a given area. But also emphasize your capacity and interest in learning about new phases of your work. Point out your desire to "grow."

During interviews, be certain to ask what would be expected of you on a day-to-day basis. Inquire about the firm's policies for advancement and raises. Do not be afraid to inquire about the fiscal solvency of the firm. Have a few specific questions prepared that will show that you have knowledge of your field and are aware enough to wish to alert yourself to potential pitfalls in the new position. You must ask why the position has become open. If someone was unhappy with the job, you must inquire why. This inquiry need not be negativistic in tone, but failure to ask will make you appear very "hungry" for the position.

At the conclusion of an interview, thank the interviewer for his time. You may write a one- or two-line note of thanks. Indicate that you look forward to hearing from the firm. Keep it brief so that you will not appear overly anxious.

During interviews it is normal to be nervous. If your voice cracks at some point, or if your thoughts get momentarily jumbled, say straightforwardly that you are "somewhat nervous." This is assertive behavior. You are expressing an honest feeling.

COGNITIVE THERAPY FOR TREATMENT OF DEPRESSION

Self-Defeating Thought	Type of Error	Rational Alternative
1. There's nothing I can do.	Catastrophizing, minimizing, stabilizing	"I can't think of anything to do right now, but if I work at it I may."
2. I'm no good.	Internalizing, globalizing, stabilizing	"I did something I regret, but that doesn't make me evil or less valuable."
3. This is absolutely awful!	Catastrophizing	"This is pretty bad, but it's not the end of the world."
4. I just don't have the brains for college.	Stabilizing, globalizing, catastrophizing	"I guess I really need to go back over the basics in that course."
5. I just can't believe I did something so disgusting!	Catastrophizing	"That was a bad experience. Well, I won't be likely to try that again."
6. I can't imagine ever feeling right again.	Stabilizing, catastrophizing	"This is painful, but if I try to work it through step by step, I'll probably eventually see my way through it."
7. It's all my fault.	Internalizing	"I'm not blameless, but I wasn't the only one involved."
8. I can't do anything right.	Globalizing, stabilizing, catastrophizing, minimizing	"I sure goofed this up, but I've done a lot of things well."
9. I hurt everybody who gets close to me.	Internalizing, globalizing, stabilizing	"I'm not totally blameless, but I'm not responsible for the whole world. Adults can be responsible for themselves."
10. If people knew the real me, they would hate me.	Globalizing, minimizing, the positive	"I'm not perfect, but nobody's perfect. I have positive features as well as negative features. Most people do."

Steps in Cognitive Therapy:

Take a look at the four people pictured below--persons A, B, C, and D--and then rate them according to the scales underneath. For instance, if you find person A to be extremely poised, place the letter A in the space next to "poised." If you find person A to be extremely awkward, place the A next to "awkward." If A impresses you as being equally poised or awkward, or if you are unsure, place the A in the center space. Once you have rated person A on the fourteen scales, repeat the process for persons B, C, and D. It is perfectly permissible to place more than one letter in the same space. This will simply mean that you gave two or more people similar ratings on the scales.

poised	__ : __ : __ : __ : __ : __ : __	awkward
modest	__ : __ : __ : __ : __ : __ : __	vain
strong	__ : __ : __ : __ : __ : __ : __	weak
interesting	__ : __ : __ : __ : __ : __ : __	boring
self-assertive	__ : __ : __ : __ : __ : __ : __	submissive
sociable	__ : __ : __ : __ : __ : __ : __	unsociable
independent	__ : __ : __ : __ : __ : __ : __	dependent
warm	__ : __ : __ : __ : __ : __ : __	cold
genuine	__ : __ : __ : __ : __ : __ : __	artificial
kind	__ : __ : __ : __ : __ : __ : __	cruel
exciting	__ : __ : __ : __ : __ : __ : __	dull
sexually warm	__ : __ : __ : __ : __ : __ : __	sexually cold
sincere	__ : __ : __ : __ : __ : __ : __	insincere
sensitive	__ : __ : __ : __ : __ : __ : __	insensitive

Done? All right, now answer a few questions. Which man (A or D) and which woman (B or C) will be:

. More likely to hold a prestigious job?   A or D? B or C?
. More likely to be divorced?   A or D? B or C?
. More likely to be a good parent?   A or D? B or C?
. More likely to experience deep personal   A or D? B or C?
  fulfillment?

A

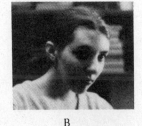
B

C

D